MEMORIES

OF

MOUNT ST. HELENS

JIM ERICKSON

THE
History
PRESS

Published by The History Press
Charleston, SC
www.historypress.com

Copyright © 2020 by Jim Erickson
All rights reserved

Front cover, bottom: Night shot of Mount St. Helens from David Johnston Observatory. *Gregg M. Erickson photo*.

First published 2020

Manufactured in the United States

ISBN 9781467145015

Library of Congress Control Number: 2019954294

Dedicated to my wife, Pam, and sons, Keith and Gregg,
for their love, support and inspiration.

CONTENTS

CONTENTS

PREFACE

I n late 2018, I entertained the notion of writing a book about Mount St. Helens, the biggest story I covered in my career as a journalist. I had visions of what it would contain: I would present my memories and accounts of the stories I wrote. I would ask a colleague, Kerry Webster, to offer his thoughts and memories about his stories. Webster willingly accepted. I would contact people who were still alive to bring their stories up to date. I did that by reaching key individuals, including Carolyn Driedger of the U.S. Geological Survey; Shirley Rosen, the niece of Harry Truman who died at his lodge on Spirit Lake; Virginia Dale, noted botanist who has studied the plant life coming back to a stark landscape; Dick Ford, the Weyerhaeuser forester who was the hero of reforestation of the volcano; and others. One of those others was especially important, namely, former president Jimmy Carter.

In January 2019, I began reading clips of my stories from the *Tacoma News Tribune*, as well as other volcano articles from the *Oregonian* and the *Columbian*, the only newspapers I had access to during the weeks I spent in Vancouver, Washington, with geologists. In February, I wrote a letter to President Carter in Plains, Georgia, including a copy of my story about his visit to the volcano to establish my credibility. My request was for his memories. After a month and a half, Carter did respond, giving me permission to use his diary entry for the day of his 1980 visit. I was elated. It inspired me to contact all the other people I interviewed for my book. I collected photos to augment the book and was pleased when The History Press accepted my proposal.

But why write the book at all? Maybe this account of a meeting I initiated with *Tacoma News Tribune* editor Don Pugnetti will shed some light on my objective. In late 1980, I suggested that the newspaper should figure out a way to be nominated for a Pulitzer Prize for what I thought was incredible Mount St. Helens coverage. Pugnetti and I examined the potential categories and determined the only possibility was "Local News." Unfortunately, the story was more "local" to the *Longview Daily News*, located in a city in closer proximity to the volcano than us. We backed off. Do you know who won the Pulitzer? The *Longview Daily News*. And deservedly so. We did enter our volcano stories in the Sigma Delta Chi (now called the Society of Professional Journalists) Northwest competition and won a first-place award. We felt vindicated somewhat. Kerry Webster and I were featured in a photo on the *Tacoma News Tribune*'s front page announcing the award because most of the volcano stories were written by us.

Now's the right time, forty years later. That's a long period in a human life but merely a blink of an eye geologically for the earth and volcanoes like Mount St. Helens. It's a good story that needs to be told.

—Jim Erickson
September 2019

ACKNOWLEDGEMENTS

Throughout my life, I have been interested in the outdoors, even longing for the chance, while living my youth in North Dakota, to visit the mountains I could see to the west in Montana. There have been so many people who inspired me to study natural science in college. In retrospect, it seems like it was a good fit with my journalism degree, helping me to communicate with earth scientists and translate their words and studies into palatable news stories for readers. That said, it is important to focus on those people who helped me along the way on the journey toward writing this book.

I am particularly in debt to Bob Lane, a colleague at the *Tacoma News Tribune* and a friend, for his constant prodding to "write something every day." Kudos to Virginia Lane, Bob's wife, a fantastic editor who looked at my first drafts and provided essential insight.

I am grateful to Don Pugnetti, editor of the *Tacoma News Tribune*, and to the newspaper, as well, for allowing me to cover Mount St. Helens, the most important story of my life. Thanks, also, to Kerry Webster, a fellow news reporter, for his memories. I am also thankful for the many volcano assignments on which I could team with photographer Bob Rudsit.

Of course, there are the many people I interviewed in 1980. Some have died. I am appreciative for having known and talked to them. I also give thanks to those people who gave me the opportunity to interview them again for this book. My list is as follows: Harry Truman, Shirley Rosen, David Johnston, Jack Hyde, Carolyn Driedger, A.B. Adams, Virginia Dale, Wendy

Adams, Al Eggers, Ryan O'Jerio and Dick Ford. They are the characters who make this story live on.

Thanks go to the Weyerhaeuser Company for flying me, Rudsit and Pugnetti into the area where salvaging was going on.

I am grateful to my son Keith for taking me to interview sessions with Carolyn Driedger, Shirley Rosen and Dick Ford. Thanks also for his photo of me with Mount St. Helens in the background.

I am also appreciative of my son Gregg for his photos of the dark sky at Mount St. Helens and his incredible panorama from the volcano's summit. Also, thanks for his photo of himself and Keith from the summit.

Thanks to the Cowlitz County Historical Society and Museum for information and a photo of the first Tower Bridge.

Thanks to Tom Lineham for his encouragement and support.

INTRODUCTION

Asacred mountain, beautiful and symmetrical, compared to Mount Fujiyama in Japan. Off limits to Native Americans who were tradition-bound to not venture above the tree line on this mountain that they called Loo-Wit. It had the reputation of being a smoking, fire-emitting volcano that drew people to it like a magnet. In the mid-1840s, that included Canadian artist Paul Kane, who painted an eruption that was remarkable. Explorers and mountaineers were attracted to Mount St. Helens, too. Put myself in the latter category, having climbed the volcano before it erupted in 1980. Thus, the stage has been set for a drama to play out, and there are lots of characters.

Carolyn Driedger, an accomplished geologist whom I call a friend, is alive today because of a warning she got the day before the mountain exploded on May 18.

Shirley Rosen is older today than her uncle—the eccentric but lovable Harry Truman, who operated a lodge at Spirit Lake and stayed there and died there—was at the time of his death. She has a lifetime of stories, as well as an interesting career made possible because of her book about Truman.

Virginia Dale became so famous after being the first to study the plant life's natural rebirth on the devastated landscape that she is recognized as a contributor to a Nobel Peace Prize. She's continuing research on Mount St. Helens.

Venus Dergan is alive today and an influential member of the Tacoma community because she got pulled by her hair from a debris flow that threatened her life and that of a companion after the eruption.

Dick Ford was shocked when trees around Mount St. Helens were blown down like matchsticks, so he became determined to be a key participant in the reforestation by the Weyerhaeuser Company of the land around the volcano. He also became an educator to visitors of the Forest Learning Center on the Spirit Lake Highway.

President Jimmy Carter played a role as a concerned politician willing to listen and provide federal assistance to America's devastated Pacific Northwest. Why did he let me use his diary entry? Perhaps because he saw my credibility in the news article I sent him. Maybe because my first name is the same as his. I'm not sure, but I am really glad he did.

Read on for a recap of my memories and the stories of these and other characters in a real-life mountain drama.

PART I
BEFORE 1980

GEOLOGICALLY, ST. HELENS' CONE WAS THE YOUNGEST IN THE CASCADES

Symmetrical and gorgeous, attractive to the eye, young and vibrant. All those descriptions perfectly fit Mount St. Helens before the great explosion on May 18, 1980, tore off 1,300 feet of its cone, including its north face. It was probably the most aesthetically pleasing mountain in the entire Cascade Range before the eruption because its upper cone was formed over the past 2,500 years, a mere blink of an eye in geological time, and was situated on an older volcanic core dating back almost 40,000 years. Its youthful, snow-covered, conical beauty was compared to that of Mount Fujiyama in Japan.

Despite being an adolescent due to its relatively new top, the volcano was complex as a result of its history, which shaped its older, ancestral cone. Judging from the amount of debris it scattered over the countryside, Mount St. Helens was the most explosive volcano in the Pacific Northwest. Geologists determined the oldest products of its ancestral eruptive phase to include a pumice layer dated to 37,600 years ago and a weathered mudflow deposit dated to 36,000 years ago.

Furthermore, scientists reported, glacial sediments of the earlier mountain from 18,000 to 14,000 years ago indicated that Mount St. Helens had at least one period of glaciation. The chemical composition marked the difference between lavas of the ancestral cone and newer cone. The earlier vent consistently erupted a variety of dacite and andesite until about 2,500 years ago. The newer, evolving cone released olivine basalt,

Mount St. Helens before 1980 with Spirit Lake in foreground. *U.S. Geological Survey (USGS) photo.*

dacite and pyroxene andesite—the three sediments making up most of the pre-1980 eruptive volcano. Scientists studying the mountain in the 1970s learned that over the past 18,000 years, Mount St. Helens has repeatedly erupted glowing avalanches of hot gas and pyroclastic debris, explosion-shattered rock fragments and showers of ash carried by winds as far away as Banff Park in Alberta, Canada. Prior to 1980, known eruptions over approximately 4,000 years can be clustered into four groups: 2500 to 1600 BC, 1200 to 800 BC, 400 BC to AD 400 and AD 1300 through the first half of the nineteenth century.

The nineteenth century has perhaps been the most interesting period of geological history because there are recorded incidents of visual observation of the eruptive nature of Mount St. Helens. In his narrative of an expedition to the Oregon Territory published in 1845, explorer Charles Wilkes reported interviewing Chief Cornelius of the Spokane tribe who remembered being awakened as a boy in 1800 by his mother, who called out to him "that the world was falling to pieces." The chief said his people were crying in terror as ash was falling very thick, accumulating to a depth of six inches, causing some to suppose that the end of the world was at hand. It was ash from an eruption of Mount St. Helens.

The first eyewitness account came in 1835 when Dr. Meredith Gairdner, who was then the official physician for the Hudson's Bay Company at Fort Vancouver, observed an eruption of the volcano. The eruption ended his proposed climb of the mountain, but his health was a factor, too. Ill with tuberculosis, he was to die two years later in Hawaii.

The doctor, from Edinburgh, sent a letter to the *Edinburgh New Philosophical Journal*, and it was published in January 1836. He reported that he had observed the eruption, noting, "There was no earthquake or preliminary noise." He wrote that the first thing that got his attention was "a dense haze for two or three days, accompanied with a fall of minute flocculi of ashes." When the haze cleared, Gairdner said he was able to see with field glasses that "the mountain was destitute of its cover of everlasting snow, and furrowed deeply by what appeared to be lava streams." Gairdner surmised, based on this incident, that there likely was an eruption in 1831, when a much denser darkness had occurred, "but no one thought to examine the appearance of the mountain."

In late 1842, Mount St. Helens began a violent eruptive phase that continued intermittently for fifteen years. The initial outbursts coincided with a reversal of normal wind patterns. Prevailing westerly or southwesterly winds had carried most of the volcano's historic eruptions north of the peak. This time, north-northwesterly currents carried a rain of ash to the south and east of the volcano. Reports from eyewitnesses along the Columbia River told of vast columns of smoke and fire shooting up and ash falling from the heavens. Father J.B.Z. Bolduc of the Cowlitz Mission wrote to his superiors in Quebec that a mountain "in the shape of a cone outside my dwelling opened one of its sides with an eruption of smoke such that all have never seen the equal to it. These eruptions of smoke took place for several days at intervals not far apart, after which eruptions of flames began." Other missionaries in the area reported similar observations.

The volcano remained active, and others observed its activity over the years. It was fortuitous that Canadian artist Paul Kane learned of Mount St. Helens' fireworks. On a journey from Toronto, Kane had been painting Indians, wildlife and scenic landscapes. He arrived near Mount St. Helens in late March 1847. On the twenty-six of that month, from a point where he had an unimpeded view of the volcano, he had begun a preliminary sketch when the mountain emitted a stream of white smoke. His finished painting is on display in the Royal Ontario Museum of Archaeology in Toronto. It is romanticized, showing a group of Indians watching a brilliant night eruption. While the natives in their canoe may not have been there for Kane

Paul Kane, a Canadian artist, visited the Northwest in 1847. The result was his painting of a nighttime eruption of Mount St. Helens. *Courtesy Royal Ontario Museum.*

to paint, the consensus is that he precisely depicted the location of Mount St. Helens' eruptive vent, thus proving that he had to have seen an actual eruption during his time spent there. The mountain stayed in eruptive mode until 1857 and then went into a lull. But it was only a matter of time before Mount St. Helens would wake up again.

FROM THE BEGINNING, MOUNT ST. HELENS WAS PART OF NATIVE AMERICAN LORE

A long time ago in a world far different than today, mountains ruled the Pacific Northwest. Native Americans, the Coast Salish tribes, who had arrived most likely over a land bridge between today's northern Asia and Alaska some twelve to twenty thousand years ago, lived in the forests and on the beaches and survived the last ice age hunkered down along the unfrozen coasts of British Columbia and perhaps even Washington State. Discovery in 2017 of an ancient settlement dated at fourteen thousand years old along the Canadian coast lends credence to that likelihood. This was a time long before the Pyramids of Giza, when now-extinct mastodons and saber-toothed tigers roamed the landscape with still-existing wolves, bison and deer. Mountains such as Mount St. Helens were visible but unreachable, due to the ice.

Salish tribes existed on clams, crabs, urchins and fish (particularly salmon); plants such as bracken ferns or bulbs of blue camas; or berries such as salmonberries or huckleberries. When the melting began and glacial ice started receding, the native people ventured out and became dependent on hunting as well. Tribes moved inland, establishing villages. Mount St. Helens, a young volcano as volcanoes go, became home to a number of tribes. But the upper parts of mountains were considered sacred, and natives never set foot above the tree line.

The Chinook tribe established the Cathlapotle village at the mouth of the Lewis River and the Skilloot village near the mouth of the Cowlitz River. The Cowlitz tribe lived in various locations along the lower and middle Cowlitz

River, while others lived directly north and south of the volcano itself. The Klickitat Indians resided between Mount St. Helens, Mount Adams and the Columbia River Gorge and were closely related to the Yakamas on the east side of the Cascade Mountain Range. The Chinooks lived primarily on salmon. The Cowlitz had few good fisheries in their territory, so they depended mostly on hunting. Both tribes also collected berries and roots around St. Helens. The Klickitats and other tribes living to the east relied more heavily on plant foods, although they did some hunting.

During seasonal visits to the wooded flanks of Mount St. Helens, members of these tribes set up temporary camps from which to embark on trips to gather plants, fish or hunt. But only a few, youths on spiritual quests, ventured higher than timberline. But no farther. Not above the trees. Spirit Lake was off limits, with native people believing that salmon in the waters were the ghosts of the evilest humans who ever lived. Tempting fate might result in punishment wreaked back on the tribes. Each tribe in the vicinity of Mount St. Helens had its own name for the peak and its own legends based on the mountain's history—usually similar themes with some slight differences. Names included Lawelatla ("One from Whom Smoke Comes") and Tah-one-lat-clah ("Fire Mountain").

Spirit Lake was surrounded by trees before the eruption, as Mount Rainier stood tall in the background. *USGS photo.*

Mount St. Helens plays a vital part in Native American lore with what is considered the most revered story passed down through generations of Coast Salish people. That legend involves Loo-Wit (Mount St. Helens) and focuses on the tale of the Bridge of the Gods and the creation of the Columbia Gorge. In most versions, Wy-east (Mount Hood) and Pahto or Klickitat (Mount Adams) are the sons of the Great Spirit, and they wage a battle over a beautiful female mountain. The brothers shake the earth, block the sunlight, throw fire at each other, burn the forests, drive off the animals and cover with ash the plants needed by the people.

The Cascade Range cracks during the fight, creating a canyon and a tunnel filled by the emptying of a huge lake east of the mountains. The Great Spirit returns. Furious, he places the Bridge of the Gods, a stone arch over the Columbia River, as a monument to peace. Furthermore, the Great Spirit puts an elderly, weathered female mountain, Loo-wit, in control as a peacemaker. Loo-wit is the keeper of the fire, which had been stolen from atop Wy-east by Coyote the Trickster. Slowly, the brothers calm down. Their coats become white again. Green forest returns. But after many years of felicity, jealousy from deep within the brothers again erupts in battle. The earth shakes so hard that the Bridge of the Gods falls into the river.

Loo-wit battles hard to end the fight. She is badly battered in the process and collapses into the river. The Great Spirit again intervenes to stop the fray. As a reward for her bravery, Loo-wit is granted one wish. She says she wants to be young and beautiful again. The Great Spirit makes it so but insists her mind must remain old. That doesn't matter to her, as all of her friends have passed away, replaced by young upstarts. Youngest of all the mountains, she moves off by herself, away from the other peaks. In some versions of this legend, Mount St. Helens is the beautiful woman the brothers fight over. In others, she is the hot-tempered wife of Mount Hood. In another, the battle is between Mount St. Helens and Mount Rainier.

PRE-ERUPTIVE CLIMBING HISTORY
INCLUDES ASCENT BY AUTHOR

Mount St. Helens was climbed numerous times from the north and south sides and other routes prior to its big eruption in May 1980, and I'm part of the pre-eruptive history, having reached its summit via the north face in 1974.

The first ascent of the mountain was recorded in August 1853 by a group of four men led by Thomas J. Dryer, founder of the *Oregonian* newspaper. Progress reports were published in the newspaper. The adventure began by following a military trail north from Vancouver, Washington, with horses to the south side of Mount St. Helens. Dryer said the party, including "Messrs. Wilson, Smith and Drew," then climbed the south slope on foot, an experience he noted was "sublimely grand and impossible to describe." Dryer said little more about the ascent than "the higher we ascended, the more difficult our progress." Reaching what he called the "highest pinnacle of the mountain," Dryer said, "the distant ocean was plainly seen." He was referring to the Pacific Ocean less than one hundred miles away. The next known climb was in 1874, and other ascents followed. In 1883, the first woman made the summit. The Oregon Alpine Club was considered the first outdoor organization to climb the mountain, reaching the summit in July 1889. The first climb of the north side in August 1893 was claimed by a party of four led by Colonel Frederick Plummer and guided by the Indian Leschi, who broke with native tradition and made the summit. While the feat was mostly accepted, there was some skepticism because the group did not sign an existing summit register. Others climbed it thereafter, including various routes on the north face. One reported a treacherous descent at night with twenty-five people clutching a single rope on the steepest ice. In August 1908, noted mountaineer Charles E. Forsyth led seven other Mazama climbers to save the life of a man, part of a trio that had crossed the mountain and was descending the south side when a rock struck the unfortunate adventurer and broke his leg. After his companions found the Mazamas camped at Spirit Lake, the combined forces hiked around to the south side, where the injured man was carried from timberline, almost over the top of the mountain and then down the north side. Such an epic rescue deserved some recognition, which occurred with the naming of the Forsyth Glacier in the Mazama group leader's honor.

Fred Beckey, author of the *Cascade Alpine Guide: Columbia River to Stevens Pass*, as well as two additional guide books of other sections of the Cascade Range, noted that because Mount St. Helens has "so few distinguishable features," little other traceable climbing history was created thereafter. By 1910, the Dog's Head, a prominent feature on the mountain's north face overlooking the Forsyth Glacier, had become part of the most popular route to the summit. Because the south side route was considered nontechnical, it was termed "kindergarten" by veteran mountaineers. I had the pleasure of meeting Beckey, a legendary climber with hundreds of first ascents in North America, in 2015 when he was in his early nineties, and it was amazing to talk to him about his experiences. Beckey died in 2017 at the age of ninety-four.

When I climbed the mountain, I was a novice climber among others with little experience who had worked to get in shape, trained to learn climbing skills and were led by veteran mountaineers who knew what they were doing. Mount St. Helens isn't truly steep. In fact, George Gibbs, an early explorer and geologist, noted that "the steepest continuous face was about 40 degrees." But we knew about the deceptive dangers of the mountain: the symmetrical likeness of the slopes invited navigation errors during periods of poor visibility, crevasses open or hidden near or in the crater increased risks, avalanches could possibly bring deep snow down on us and slips on steep ice could result in falls of long distances. Not ever having been on St. Helens' slopes before, I was filled with apprehension during the drive down Interstate 5 and along State Route 504, the Spirit Lake Highway. Parking at Timberline, we got out our backpacks and gear, put on boots and began hiking, taking the climbers' upslope trail for a mile or so and gaining altitude. Keeping to the left, with the Forsyth Glacier always in sight, we finally attained Dog's Head, a buttress at roughly 7,700 feet. This shoulder on the mountain's north flank overlooked the Forsyth Glacier. The Dog's Head was our overnight resting spot. We put up tents, cooked our meals and prepared for the night. And what a night it was on this exposed escarpment. The wind picked up and blew constantly with fierce intermittent gusts that really shook the tent. My tent was anchored down and I was inside with my gear, but I still felt insecure. I harbored thoughts that the tent anchors would pull out and my tent would blow off Dog's Head with me in it. That didn't happen, fortunately.

In the morning, the wind had died down, but we were tired without much sleep during the windy ordeal, and we still had a climb to the summit facing us. I looked out of my tent and saw a companion's tent, which had only one support pole to begin with, totally collapsed with him inside. We got breakfast going, took out what we needed for snack food and water on the summit climb, plus compass and extra clothing, and put them in our day packs. We took our tents down and got our backpacks ready to go down once we returned from the summit. Our trip leaders wanted to make the summit effort more entertaining, so they decided to take us up and through the Forsyth Glacier rather than an easier slog to the east of Dog's Head. We were roped together in teams of three or four. We started upward and ventured onto the Nelson Glacier. After about 300 feet of elevation gain, we moved westward onto the Forsyth Glacier. We encountered some crevasses that we either circumnavigated, stepped over or crossed on a snow bridge. Huge seracs dwarfed us in some spots, and we carefully negotiated around a deep bergschrund around 9,100 feet. We made the summit at 9,677 feet and rested in the crater under Chimney Rock.

Our return trip was less eventful because we knew what to expect. Being roped together helped us descend smoothly, alleviating the fear of falling forward. Afterward, we felt fulfilled that Mount St. Helens allowed us to attain the summit. Confidence built on this success, I went on to climb Mount Rainier, which is 14,411 feet high, and other peaks before 1980.

PART II

THE MOUNTAIN AWAKENS

THE SLUMBER OVER,
THE MOUNTAIN SOFTLY RUMBLED

Mount St. Helens awoke from a 123-year sleep on March 20, 1980, with a shiver. A comparatively light earthquake measuring 4.1 on the Richter scale and not felt outside the immediate vicinity of the volcano was recorded by the lone seismic station positioned on the west flank of the mountain near the tree line. That information was transmitted to the University of Washington seismic center in Seattle. The quake, on a Friday, was followed by more seismic activity the next two days and got scientists interested. Earthquakes, primarily in the 3.0 to 4.0 range, came faster and faster. Scientists from the University of Washington and the U.S. Geological Survey (USGS) rushed to install newly obtained earthquake metering devices around St. Helens. A young, enthusiastic geologist just on the scene, David Johnston, nattily attired in suit, tie and street shoes, volunteered to take them to the mountain. Scientists wanted to gain more data to see if their hunches were right—that volcanic activity was imminent. As a precaution, due to possible quake-triggered avalanches on the mountain's slopes, the area around St. Helens was closed to the public on March 23.

On March 27 in the early afternoon, the mountain proved scientists right. An explosion heard throughout southwest Washington resulted in emissions of sulfurous gas and ash rising above the clouds. With a break in the clouds, a news team from the *Columbian* spotted a hole near the north part of the summit during a flight. Two days later, as emissions continued, scientists flying over the peak spotted a second crater. They estimated one was 300 feet by 450 feet and the other 90 feet by 150 feet with each 60 to 90 feet deep, with a small 30-foot bridge between. Blue flame was seen in the small crater, and blue-colored lightning was arcing between the craters. Scientists had speculated that hot molten lava (magma) might have triggered the eruption, but geologist Bob Christensen said, "It is not a glow associated with the presence of magma." Ash sullied what had been pristine white snow on the mountain's slopes.

A plane carrying photographer Bob Rudsit and me from the *Tacoma News Tribune* also recorded the twin craters on the peak's summit and ash blanketing the snow. Unfortunately, we were among a host of news teams and scientists clogging the airspace around the mountain, causing the Federal Aviation Administration to impose special restrictions on the airspace. So many tourists came to view the volcano that highways quickly became jammed, and law enforcement officers began to fear that evacuation would become impossible if a severe eruption occurred.

News of St. Helens' eruption spread around the world. Closer to its flanks, however, people were filled with feelings of bewilderment mixed with bits of humor. "Volcano?" snapped S.T. Lee, owner of the Kid Valley Store, as he thumped the top of the candy counter. "Hell, somebody just made that up. There ain't no volcano." The humor, however, was more a reflection of the tension and sense of uncertainty being felt by the mountain's human neighbors. They couldn't feel, hear or see the mountain's activity all the time, but they knew they were living in the shadow of a mountain that might become very deadly indeed. Geologists risked the danger to land on the mountain's slopes in helicopters to dash in and collect gas and ash samples for experiments and analysis. Occasionally, an eruption would toss boulders and chunks of ice hundreds of feet into the air.

By early April, ongoing eruptions resulted in the collapse of the bridge between the two craters, turning the two into one the size of seven football fields long and two football fields deep. The summit of St. Helens looked like a battleground that had been bombarded by artillery and bombers. Covered with ash of its own eruptions, the mountain had changed from its usual white spring mantle to a cloak of dirty gray and black. The walls of the single yawning crater slanted deeply down inside the peak like rocky funnels. Ash, pumice and rock mixed with huge blocks of ice along the sides and bottom. Heat from eruptions melted snow and ice and created small lakes at the bottom. Some feared increased runoff from the mountain would cause flooding, but power reservoirs along the rivers had been lowered to a level that officials said could hold back a huge torrent if St. Helens' snow melted rapidly. On April 3, scientists noticed the first "harmonic tremors." Unlike

Ash blanketed the volcano during wake-up activity in March 1980. *Author's photo.*

Twin craters were created at the beginning of renewed emissions. *Author's photo.*

normal earthquakes with sharp, abrupt movements, these quakes were undulating ripples indicative of red-hot lava moving inside the mountain. While dozens of scientists were elated about their newest natural laboratory, law enforcement officials in towns and counties near the mountain took a substantially less excited view of the proceedings. Implementation of safety zones and roadblocks was futile. Hundreds of tourists found that a maze of logging roads crisscrossing the area was not patrolled and offered easy access to areas providing closer views of the mountain. Hard-pressed police and sheriff's deputies had been working twelve-hour shifts. Cowlitz and Skamania County officials asked for National Guard assistance, and Washington governor Dixy Lee Ray granted the request. Even so, the logging roads remained open. It would have taken twenty-nine roadblocks, authorities claimed, to cut off all traffic to the mountain, and they only had manpower to block six principal roads.

Someone who was particularly persistent had a good chance of getting close to the mountain and doing something daring. One of those who did just that was Fred Miller of Seattle. Upon returning from the summit, the ash-covered mountaineer had one word for his experience: "intense." The volcano puffed steam and ash while he was on top of the peak, Miller said.

Wind-swept snow gave an eerie tone to the mountain's summit in April 1980. *Author's photo.*

"It was like a dust storm. I couldn't see my feet." He wasn't the only brazen adventurer. A climbing crew ascended the crater rim with movie cameras to film commercials for two brands of beer. Most of those taking chances, however, had more sensible reasons for being there—scientists collecting samples of ash, rock and gases or news teams collecting photographs, film and news accounts from the mountain.

In Cougar, a town at the base of the peak's south side, local residents complained the roadblocks were cutting off the usual trade of fishermen and hikers critical to the town's livelihood. Authorities finally gave in and opened the road to Cougar. People from as far away as Montana and South Carolina streamed into the town. Kerry Webster, a fellow reporter at the *Tacoma News Tribune*, remembers the flow of folks from far afield drawn to Mount St. Helens. He said one person named Mike Goodell, a firefighter from Portland, Oregon, who traveled on his day off, was clutching a pair of binoculars with one hand and a can of Coors in the other, gazing at the volcano and pleading, "C'mon, baby, do your thing," punctuating his call with a soulful swig from the beer can. Obligingly, the mountain puffed a cloud of steam and ash into the slanting rays of the late afternoon sun. "Awr-r-right!" he shouted, screwing the binoculars deep into his eye sockets. "Lookit that! Lookit that!" A cricket-like chorus of camera shutters rose from the two dozen other volcano-watchers lining the shoulder of Highway 503 at Yale Lake.

Ron Nelson and Ralph Philson had come a far piece to see the activity. The computer engineers had flown into Portland from Columbia, South Carolina, on business and found themselves with time to kill. "We just rented a car and boogied on up," drawled Nelson. "We don't have any volcanoes in South Carolina." "No mountains to speak of either," laughed Philson.

Dave and Julie Wang, from Butte, Montana, were on their way home from Reno, Nevada, when they learned about the volcano and decided to take a little detour. "It's a once-in-a-lifetime thing," said Dave, a pilot for an air pollution agency. Somebody said jokingly he should cite the volcano. Wang grinned.

Oregonians Scott Braman and Sharon Potterf had a six-hundred-millimeter astronomical telescope focused on the mountain. "It's pretty exciting," Braman said. "Through the telescope we can see the cracks in the snow and the ash ripples down the side."

Charles Ragland, another Oregonian, was propped comfortably on the hood of his station wagon, a pillow under his head and a can of vegetable juice at his side, scanning the mountain through binoculars. "Why did I come? Well, I just wanted to, that's all," he shrugged. "I came for the solar eclipse last year, too."

Senior citizens Fair Ekroth and her husband, Nels, had come from Seattle because they had fond memories of Mount St. Helens. "I feel like I've come to visit a dear friend in the hospital, and I don't know whether it's going to be terminal," Fair said sadly.

With that show over, the mountain settled into a quiet mode for a few weeks, sputtering intermittently. The scientists and other agencies faced another problem: they were beginning to run out of money. Watching over a volcano, they discovered, was an expensive proposition. The USGS was spending $2,000 a day to simply house and feed its scientists. In addition, there were the geologists' salaries and costs of chartering helicopters for close-up looks at the mountain in the amount of $300 an hour. The U.S. Forest Service indicated its extra expenses had risen past $150,000 and were growing at the rate of $9,000 a day. The Washington National Guard, State Patrol and Department of Emergency Services were all spending thousands over their budgets. Cowlitz and Skamania Counties, charged with keeping the hordes of tourists away, were rapidly running over their budgets, too.

As April was winding down, a U-2 spy plane flying high above the volcano with infrared cameras in its belly took photographs that revealed the existence of hot spots within the mountain's flanks. The hot spots, scientists insisted, meant that magma, the molten rock that becomes lava, was rising in the mountain's innards. On April 30 they reported that delicate instruments mounted on the slopes of the volcano indicated a bulge was developing on the north side of the peak. Pressing outward a few inches at a time, the bulge provided confirmation of incredible geologic pressure building within the mountain's fiery core. Mount St. Helens slipped into a period of quietude. No eruptions were reported for two weeks. The calm was dangerously deceptive, though. Outwardly, the only sign of life from the volcano was the steady trickling of water off the volcano's slopes. Deep inside its core, the mountain was ticking like a time bomb, ready to explode. "It's not if, but when the volcano goes up," said a worried Cowlitz County sheriff Les Nelson. "I've never wanted to be wrong about anything more in my life, but there's pressure being built up inside the mountain and it's got to go somewhere."

The mountain undisputedly was moving. Like some unearthly monster from a horror movie, the bulge grew inexorably outward. It stretched across the northerly face of the mountain from the steaming summit downward as much as three thousand or four thousand feet. Areas well known to mountaineers and tourists alike had shifted. The Dog's Head, a rock outcropping near the Forsyth Glacier, and Sugar Bowl, at about six thousand feet on the peak's northeast flank, had moved by a few inches, geologists said. Goat Rocks, a ridge nearby, had moved five feet to the north of where it had been. The balloon-like bulge was believed to be caused by lava moving upward inside the volcano. Geologists conceded that the bulge dangerously increased the possibilities of severe avalanches on that side of the peak.

State officials asked Governor Ray to order areas around the mountain closed. The governor complied, creating a "red zone" and a "blue zone" beyond that. Schoolchildren in nearby towns celebrated Ray's order. They held a volcano evacuation drill. Scientists remained worried. Standing in the Timberline parking lot with the mountain's north face before me, other media and gawkers, David Johnston offered a warning: "I have a gut feeling that as the bulge continues to grow something dramatic is going to happen. You shouldn't be here. You should go now." All of us did, but I wondered in my own mind, biting my tongue for not asking him, "Then why are you here?" But I knew the answer. Johnston was taking calculated risks to get scientific data to help everyone determine what the volcano was going to do. I was there, taking risks, too, for the same reason: to let people know what was happening in the biggest story I had ever covered.

Ironically, the phenomenon of the bulge that worried scientists generated a mixed mood among nearby residents who had lived with the hassles and hubbub of an active volcano for six weeks. "I think people are getting kind of tired of it now," said a clerk at tiny Cougar's lone grocery store. "They want to go back and have their lives. The novelty has worn off." Some just wanted nothing to do with the peak. "She's going to blow," predicted a resident of the small town of Yacolt. "I feel it in my bones," he added, "and when she blows, she's going to take a thousand feet right off the top of her." As if to punctuate his statements, on May 7, Mount St. Helens blew its first steam and ash eruptions in two weeks, but it was not the huge bang that some had expected. Three emissions occurred late that day, from 5:57 to 6:10 p.m., 6:23 to 6:30 p.m. and 10:26 to 11:36 p.m. Plumes rose to thirteen thousand feet above sea level, about four hundred feet higher than the peak's summit. The eruptions were similar to previous episodes in early and mid-April.

Something was happening inside the volcano, though. It was percolating like a near-boiling coffee pot. Earthquakes grew in intensity, frequently surpassing 5.0 on the Richter scale. The north face bulge continued to heave. Harmonic tremors were shaking the peak, strong indications that molten lava was moving upward inside the volcano.

While many scientists wondered about what all that might mean in terms of a future eruption, Tacoma's Al Eggers willingly shared his theory, even though he stopped short of making an outright prediction. Eggers, a University of Puget Sound (UPS) geologist and professor, had noticed that there was a relationship between earth tides and volcanic eruptions at other mountains. In general, remarked Eggers, his research had convinced him that the highest chance of eruptions occurred when tides were at their minimum. When would the next minimum period occur? Checking a computer printout of tide tables, he told me, "Well, maybe about May 21." Eggers missed by only three days.

HARRY R. TRUMAN, A LEGENDARY MAN OF THE MOUNTAIN

When we reached the end of the Spirit Lake Highway, we came upon a magnificent log lodge, perhaps a hundred feet long and two stories high with roof dormers. Pathways led to about a dozen cabins. A dock a hundred yards away on Spirit Lake was cluttered with dozens of rowboats, motorboats and canoes tied to them, ready for use. Mount St. Helens, an iconic Cascade mountain, towered above the lake in all its splendor, despite some recent volcanic emissions that had sprinkled ash on its usually white flanks. A sign outside the lodge broadcasted "Mount St. Helens Lodge" with Harry Truman's name emblazoned below. His lodge was a mile from the mountain as the crow flies. On this April morning in 1980, *Tacoma News Tribune* photographer Bruce Kellman and I found Harry Randall Truman outside his lodge feeding several of his sixteen cats that roamed the place at will. He was going about business as usual, although there were few guests these days because of the danger of the volcano. Truman led the way inside a side door to what he termed his "cocktail lounge," a grouping of chairs and tables, a counter with stools and a bar. He made himself a whiskey and Coke. We declined his offer for drinks, saying we were on duty. He plunked down in a chair in front of a window facing the mountain and put binoculars to his eyes to peer out at the 9,677-foot peak.

"The face I look at hasn't changed much from what I can tell," Truman remarked. "The contours seem pretty much the same. I can't see the other side, but it appears the northeast ridge has changed some." Truman lived up to his reputation as a character loaded with colorful metaphors, making it

Harry Truman loved sitting on the porch of his lodge at Spirit Lake and vowed never to leave in the face of a volcano's eruption. And he didn't. *Courtesy of Shirley Rosen.*

somewhat difficult to quote him in a family newspaper. He certainly did no injustice to the "give 'em hell" label of his presidential namesake.

He lambasted the scientists studying the mountain: "They don't know any more about the mountain than I do. And they admit it. I know one thousand times more about the outside of the mountain than they do. Who else has watched her movements for fifty-four years?"

The eighty-three-year-old Truman recommended to the scientists that they "drop bombs on the mountain to clean it out so it will never erupt again."

But Truman explained that the scientists told him they couldn't bother nature. "Now why the hell not?" Truman exclaimed. "Why can't we fool with nature. It's fooling with us."

When I told Truman that officials had considered bombardment of Mount Etna in Italy a few years earlier to let out and divert lava, Truman expressed a bit of surprise, stating, "Damn, I thought that was my idea."

I asked him if he thought the general public would have been upset had Mount St. Helens been bombed. He shrugged and shook his head, noting, "With the type of TV shows out there, I think the public can handle anything." Truman maintained that the public was ravenous for an eruption of catastrophic proportions. "They want the mountain to destroy everything and to see bodies, including mine, floating down the Toutle River," he said. "The public is really morbid. What a bunch of silly asses."

Truman vowed to "live to be 110 just to spite all those people who want me to die."

Truman was adamant about staying put because Spirit Lake was his home, and he just couldn't live anywhere else. Or die anywhere else. Although he was the only person living in the vicinity of what was America's newest active volcano, he was hardly alone. He was inundated by dozens of newspaper and television news teams. That included me and Kellman.

"One day there were three helicopters lined up on the road and many more news vehicles," Truman recounted. "There was a crew from NBC-TV out there, and I was on the *Today Show* the next morning. I've had others, too, including a guy from the *Baltimore Sun*, and it was cloudy and he didn't even get to see the mountain."

In response to the flood of news coverage, Truman received such an outpouring of mail that he couldn't keep up with reading it all. "I've heard from New Orleans, Hawaii, Australia, and I'll hear from England sure as hell," he said. "It's the funniest damn thing."

But Truman was anything but starstruck by the newfound attention, telling me that he was "quite a boy before all this."

Why was that, I asked him.

"Well," he asserted, "I've been here more than fifty years, that's why. I've had a million-dollar layout here—lodge, cabins, boats." Truman came to Spirit Lake in 1926, hiking in the last mile on snowshoes. He built a cabin and lived off the land. In 1929, he built a home and erected tent frames that he rented to campers and fishermen. In 1937, sparks from a fireplace ignited a bearskin rug and totally destroyed his home. In 1939, he built his lodge. Truman walked us through the lobby with huge support beams and the dining room and motioned his hand to rooms upstairs. Two devastating windstorms in 1950 and 1962 destroyed most of his cabins, and he had to rebuild them. But he persevered and kept going, offering rooms and recreational activities to thousands of people over the years.

He was particularly pleased to talk about his very important best friend. That special person was none other than the late U.S. Supreme Court justice

William O. Douglas. "Bill and I used to go horsepacking in the Cascade Mountains together," Truman recalled. "One time, Bill bandaged my legs when I got injured." After the accident, Truman said, Douglas sent Truman a letter. One of Truman's prized possessions, the letter stated the judge's warning: "Harry, you be careful. I'll not always be around to look after you." Truman said he had no idea how prophetic the letter would be when it was written, as Douglas died shortly thereafter. A national forest in Washington State bears the judge's name.

Truman was adhering to Douglas's advice when it came to the multitude of earthquakes that began around March 1980 and continued up to Mount St. Helens' eruption. "I've been through hundreds of them," Truman said, "but they still scare the hell out of me."

His sixteen cats were terrified at first, but now "they just think I'm rocking them," he said. So the cats were not bothered at all by the shaking. Truman said some raccoons scared off by the mountain's rumblings had come back, but the birds hadn't.

"Listen," he said softly. "You cannot hear a single chirp anywhere. I miss the birds. But they'll be back."

Finally, Truman extended an invitation to come back in a year "when everything has died down." Then, the celebration could begin with his favorite whiskey and Coke drinks. He offered assurance: "I'll be here sure as hell. We'll have a Coke-high and laugh about this."

HARRY TRUMAN CERTAINLY PROVED his reputation as a crusty, stubborn character. He stayed put and was vaporized when Mount St. Helens erupted at 8:32 a.m. on Sunday, May 18, 1980. He had vowed the volcano wouldn't harm him and promised he would make "Coke-high" drinks if a news photographer and I came back in a year. And he said we could have a good "laugh about the volcano."

We returned in May 1981 and honored Truman near a downed tree–littered Spirit Lake where he had operated a lodge for more than half a century. I spoke softly, "We're here, Harry. But you're not."

We fondly remembered our time with Truman in late April 1980. Less than three weeks after that visit, Mount St. Helens erupted in a fury, pushing a powerful pyroclastic flow out of its north slope and emitting upward a towering plume of ash that spread around the world. And Harry and his lodge were gone in a flash.

A GEOLOGIST WHO DESERVED RESPECT
FOR HIS INSIGHT

Jack Hyde was a personable, intelligent Tacoma scientist considered an expert on Mount St. Helens, having studied the peak for many years. When the southwest Washington volcano became active in late March 1980, Hyde was a willing spokesman for possible scenarios even though he wasn't officially attached to the geological team located in Vancouver, Washington. He was the first to predict an explosive lateral blast was imminent because his observations showed the volcano had no apparent fumeroles. I constantly leaned on Hyde, an earth sciences instructor at Tacoma Community College, for expert analysis as the mountain continued to warm up, heading toward a possible monster eruption.

In mid- to late April, geologists noticed that the mountain was forming a large bulge on its north flank. The reason: pressure from within, perhaps caused by magma pushing upward and outward or rocks deformed by heated groundwater. Whatever the cause, it was obvious that the bulge was growing. It made the scientists monitoring the volcano uneasy, to say the least. They felt they and anyone coming up to Timberline facing the peak's north side would be extremely vulnerable to an explosion ripping directly toward them.

I remember David Johnston, working in the Timberline parking lot, telling me, other media and curious visitors that we all needed to leave. "If the mountain blows, we're going to get hit right here." Members of the media and gawkers quickly got into their vehicles and chased each other down the mountain. But I wondered in my own mind and should have asked Johnston, "Then why are you still at Timberline?"

I posed the question of the bulge and the potential lateral explosion to Hyde for a story I wrote in early May 1980, and he remarked, "I have a gut feeling that as the bulge continues to grow, something dramatic is going to happen." If the north slope of Mount St. Helens gave way, Hyde explained, the explosion would be spectacular, occurring without warning. He compared the activity of St. Helens to Mount Bezymianny, a Russian volcano on the Kamchatka Peninsula one thousand miles north of Japan.

In September 1955, Bezymianny began to shake with earthquakes and after three weeks erupted with steam and ash emissions, just like Mount St. Helens in March 1980. The wake-up call continued until March 1956, when suddenly Bezymianny exploded violently, destroying the landscape for more than twenty miles. The unique quirk about that was that Bezymianny did *not* erupt skyward, as one often sees volcanoes in photos and news videos. That Russian volcano blew out sideways, ripping the mountain apart and literally laying waste to everything in its directional path, while leaving the peripheral landscape unscathed.

If St. Helens followed the same scenario, Hyde said, the devastation would be similar to that wreaked by Bezymianny. I asked Hyde for his take on the strategy of geologists watching St. Helens' activity from observation points on nearby ridges. He paused for a moment and then offered a pensive but dire warning: "I hope they're not in a direct line. That's like looking down the barrel of a loaded gun."

Unfortunately, Hyde, I thought, was being taken as the Rodney Dangerfield of geology, and perhaps the word "danger" as part of the comedian's last name could truly be appropriate for one like Hyde, who was professing the danger of the volcano. Anyway, Hyde seemed to get little respect, in my opinion, because he was not officially part of the U.S. Geological Survey, nor was he in a position of responsibility. Consequently, his opinion was dismissed by those in authority. This despite the fact that Hyde had a doctorate in volcanology from the University of Washington, where he previously got his bachelor's degree in geology, and had worked with USGS scientists researching Cascade volcanoes, including Mount St. Helens. Two of those from USGS were legends in their field: Dwight "Rocky" Crandell and Donal Mullineaux out of the Denver office. They studied mudflows and other evidence of past eruptions. As a result of his observations, Hyde noted that St. Helens did not possess visible vents. Hyde concluded that pressure from rising magma would increase until the mountain exploded. Wherever that pressure manifested itself, a growing bulge would occur. In the case of Mount St. Helens, rising magma veered off to the north flank of the mountain. Ultimately, the lateral blast on May 18, 1980, ripped out the north face of St. Helens. David Johnston, the young geologist who died on a ridge facing the north side of the volcano, was the only scientist who believed Hyde's evaluation of the threat.

Hyde, who always expressed a concern about the environment, was active in helping preserve Tacoma's waterfront and served as an advocate for quality of life as a Tacoma city councilman from 1980 to 1989. He was mayor of Tacoma in 1994 for seventeen days before suffering a heart attack and dying. One of his first acts as mayor during his brief stint was announcing an Environmental Protection Agency–backed endeavor to clean up heavily polluted Thea Foss Waterway. In his honor, Commencement Park in Old Town Tacoma, along Ruston Way, was renamed Jack Hyde Park in 2002.

Jacque Hyde, whom I contacted in 2019, remembered her late husband's work on Mount St. Helens prior to the cataclysmic 1980 eruption. "I vividly recall three or four summers in the 1970s when Jack was working on St. Helens," she said, noting that Jack was the "first geologist to predict that St. Helens would erupt again before Mounts Rainier and Baker." She said he studied the other volcanoes too but was especially fascinated by the conical beauty of St. Helens, which he had climbed many times. "Jack was like the old man of the mountain," Jacque mused. "He was never one to say too much and took people the way they came."

DAY BEFORE ERUPTION COINCIDENCES RESULTED IN WHAT-IF MOMENTS

It was Saturday, May 17, 1980, and geologists in Vancouver were having their regular staff meeting and talking about how Mount St. Helens had calmed down. A lull before a storm, someone suggested. Because of the restful nature of the volcano, a few scientists had the weekend off. The discussion turned to a problem. David Johnston had hired Harry Glicken, a graduate student, to stay in a small white trailer on a ridge north of the mountain, a monitoring station referred to as Coldwater II. Glicken had been instructed to issue a warning if he observed an avalanche or eruption triggered by the north-side bulge exploding. Glicken needed to leave for California to address his graduate program in the fall. Who could fill in for him on Coldwater II? Don Swanson, who had been reassigned from the Hawaiian Volcano Observatory to St. Helens when it became active, volunteered to take over. After the meeting ended, Swanson realized he had a conflict. He went to Johnston and asked if Johnston could cover for him just that night. Swanson had a graduate student visiting from Germany and wanted to see him off on Sunday. Swanson vowed to replace Johnston later that day. Johnston had some legitimate fears about being so close to a volcano that could turn deadly. He was seriously concerned because the mountain's north side had bottled-up magma that was building up, creating a bulge that grew bigger and bigger. It was almost as if there was no way for the magma to escape to the surface. Johnston knew firsthand about how the unexpected could happen. He had experienced it on Alaska's Mount Augustine years before. He had scrambled to Augustine's summit to obtain some gas samples

Scientist David Johnston used a gas-detecting device on Coldwater II ridge. *USGS photo.*

and was heading back down when the mountain released a pyroclastic flow of lava and gas that chased him down the mountain. Johnston, who related to me the full story during an interview while working for the USGS on Mount St. Helens, said he dashed down the Augustine slope as quickly as he could, made it to a three-sided wooden structure halfway down the mountain and stayed there, knowing he could never outrun the hot, fiery flow. The pyroclastic flow hit the backside of the hut, split and ran in two directions on either side of the structure. A worried, anxious Johnston saw the wood walls being charred, but fortunately, because the flow was moving so fast, it did not ignite the structure. Surviving a near-death situation, Johnston was able to eventually escape down the mountain. Despite his misgivings about St. Helens, Johnston gave in, agreeing to man Coldwater II. After all, it would only be for one night. What could happen? He got into his government-issued Ford Pinto station wagon and drove up to Coldwater II. He didn't know, though, that he was going to have visitors.

Carolyn Driedger, now a prominent geologist at the David A. Johnston Cascades Volcano Observatory, remembers vividly the day before the eruption, when she and Mindy Brugman, both young scientists at the beginning of their careers, went up to Coldwater II to help Johnston. "We were in the USGS glaciology office in Tacoma," she told me, "when director Mark Meier made reference to an increase of seismic activity on the mountain and wondered if we could take a new piece of equipment to Johnston." It was a distance-measuring device using laser technology to focus on the volcano's north side to measure the bulge's growth and movement of magma beneath the surface. Driedger and Brugman agreed because it might also give them an opportunity to catch a helicopter flight to continue their study of the mountain's Shoestring Glacier. It was raining that day, Driedger recalled, and she was concerned that might hamper any flight to the glacier. But they went anyway because they were glad to be able to help Johnston. Glicken, who hadn't left yet for California, was still there. The helicopter couldn't make it, so the glacier trip was out for Driedger and Brugman. They spent a pleasant afternoon with their two colleagues, conversing and snapping photos. They took sleeping bags and gear from their car and announced they would stay the night and proceed with their work the next day. Johnston became adamant, telling them, "This is not the safest place to be. You should go. The volcano could blow right out and get us here." Driedger remembers thinking about that and restraining a question that she wanted to ask but didn't: "Then why are you here, David?" Her and Brugman's euphoria at being here at the mountain—weather clearing to create a beautiful sunset—had been shattered by Johnston's dire warning. Driedger and Brugman left, driving off into the sunset, rays of light streaking across the sky. They stopped to take one last sunset shot of the mountain behind Silver Lake. The two geologists noticed many animals jumping across the highway as they drove back toward the freeway. *I wonder what they know?* they thought. Glicken left later as night was falling.

The next morning, Driedger and Brugman attended a staff meeting in Vancouver, as suggested by Johnston. Then, they headed back toward Tacoma, where they had been based. Driving back on I-5, they saw an unbelievable sight. "There was this big black rolling cloud to the east coming from the mountain," Driedger said. "We wondered what that was. Then it dawned on us. It could be the debris avalanche David mentioned last night as a possibility. The black cloud kept moving to the north, and that was our clue." They turned their car around and headed back to Vancouver. Their hunch was confirmed once they arrived at the USGS office. The mountain had erupted. Driedger and Brugman were quickly put to work, answering phones that were ringing off the hook. They created talking points from information fed to them by other volcanologists. "We did this all day," Driedger recalled. Finally, others relieved the two young women scientists of their task. Driedger said rescue missions were launched to find Johnston. Glicken and others searched for him. Glicken was particularly anxious because it should have been him on the ridge and not Johnston. After one helicopter returned, Glicken would persuade another to take him back up. Swanson also participated in searches. The landscape was so devastated that they could hardly discern where Coldwater II had been. After returning from his first rescue mission, Swanson was in shock, Driedger said, adding, "Don's face was as white as this sheet of paper." It was ironic, Driedger noted, that eleven years after St. Helens erupted, Glicken died on a volcano in Japan. Glicken was serving as a guide for French volcanologists Katia and Maurice Krafft on Mount Unzen when the mountain erupted and the trio and thirty-nine others perished. The Kraffts had gained a reputation for their videos of volcanoes to aid disaster preparedness and were attempting to get close enough to adequately shoot a pyroclastic flow.

Forty years have passed since Mount St. Helens exploded, but Driedger still remembers Johnston. "David knew it was a hazard. Yet he was there," she opined. Driedger acknowledged it has sometimes made her second-guess the collective feeling of USGS scientists that Johnston was only taking

David Johnston relaxing at his post on May 17. *USGS photo by Harry Glicken.*

calculated risks as part of his assigned job to warn people of the dangers and that he did not have a death wish. She has resigned herself to that conclusion, too, reminding herself that in previous eruptive episodes, Mount St. Helens had never reached that ridge. "So I think David did not have a death wish," she mused. "I really believe that." The lateral blast of the mountain's north slope, however, did reach Coldwater II, and Johnston perished within minutes. A pensive Driedger shook her head, saying, "I think about David every day of my life."

PART III

THE BIG BLAST

THE DAY MOUNT ST. HELENS EXPLODED LIKE AN ATOMIC BOMB

Within minutes after receiving a phone call that Mount St. Helens had erupted at 8:32 a.m. on Sunday, May 18, 1980, I was ready and gone, catching an Amtrak train south from Tacoma to Vancouver, Washington, knowing that Interstate 5 would be clogged and I'd never make it to the Cascade Volcano Center, where scientists were monitoring the mountain. Listening to a battery-powered radio, I learned that the volcano had exploded in an eruption likened to the force greater than that of an atomic bomb. The ferocious blast ripped the mountain apart, taking more than 1,300 feet off its top, lowering its elevation from 9,677 feet to 8,363 feet. The initial explosion was heard more than two hundred miles away in the Canadian province of British Columbia, but there was no sound in proximity of the volcano in southwest Washington State.

When the train got closer to Vancouver, I was able to take some photos of the west side of the volcano. Unbelievable. When my 120-mile train ride ended, I dashed to the volcano center in downtown Vancouver and started getting information I could relay to the *Tacoma News Tribune*. Besides myself, our news team was made up of photographer Bob Rudsit in the air over the eruption; reporter Kerry Webster and photographer Russ Carmack on the ground near the volcano; reporter Marlowe Churchill and photographer Warren Anderson from the foothills of Mount Rainier to the north; photographer Bruce Kellman; and reporters Jack Pyle, Rob Tucker, Joseph Turner, Bob Lane, Jeff Weathersby, Betty Anderson, Jerry Pugnetti, Margaret Ainscough and John Gillie. What we learned was that

Mount St. Helens blew outward and upward on May 18, 1980. *USGS photo.*

the destruction was unprecedented and the numbers of dead or missing in the dozens (precise figures months later put the death total at fifty-seven). The searing explosion flattened everything in its wake north of the mountain, leveling trees and reaching ridges 8 miles away, killing Reid Blackburn, a twenty-seven-year-old photographer for the *Columbian,* and David Johnston, a thirty-year-old geologist. Johnston's last words were, "Vancouver! Vancouver! This is it!" The two were in camps a mile apart when the mountain blew. And, of course, Harry Truman, eighty-three, owner of a lodge at Spirit Lake, was killed and his resort obliterated. Spirit Lake, once a picturesque body of water, was virtually gone, choked with downed timber and boiling mud and ash.

The explosion triggered countless mudflows that raced down the north and south forks of the Toutle River, killing motorists in their cars, snapping numerous highway and railroad bridges and sweeping away homes, cars and large logging equipment rigs. Scientists in Vancouver told me they determined that two major earthquakes struck minutes apart in the area at a time when many residents were still having breakfast. Those quakes concentrated their force in the north-side bulge of ice and rock that had been growing for several weeks at a rate of about five feet a day. Something had to give, and it did. That blister of rock separated without warning,

Ash emissions could be seen from train traveling to Vancouver, Washington. *Author's photo.*

and the Goat Rocks formation on the peak was shoved westward. Pent-up force within the volcano burst forth. Geologist Dan Miller told me and other media in Vancouver that an explosion such as that had not occurred at Mount St. Helens in the past thirty-two thousand years. University of Washington seismologist Steve Malone said the eruption "surpassed everyone's worst case scenario."

Hundreds of people were evacuated from the mountain within hours. Law enforcement officials and the Washington National Guard began their efforts in the Toutle River Valley shortly after the initial eruption. Later on Sunday, they began evacuating residents along the Kalama and Lewis Rivers as the threat of floods developed. An estimated 1,800 residents fled to safer ground. At one point, the Toutle River, a well-known and productive fishing stream, was so hot from pyroclastic flows of red-hot gas and ash that fish were leaping onto the riverbanks to escape the heat, witnesses reported. The river became a sterile stream devoid of any living thing. Two major bridges on State Route 504, the Spirit Lake Highway, were destroyed: Tower Bridge seven miles east of Interstate 5 and Coal Bank Bridge at the confluence of the north and south forks of the Toutle River east of the town of Toutle. The blast scattered rocks and ice throughout the area and destroyed all vegetation between St.

Left: The land around the peak to the north was virtually destroyed. *Author's photo.*

Below: Blown-down timber in Green Valley north of the volcano looked like matchsticks. *USGS photo.*

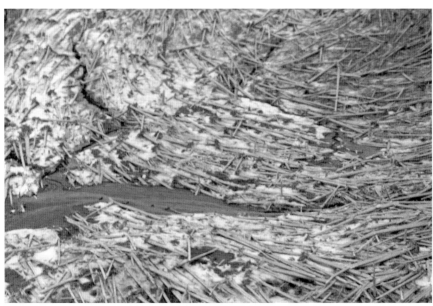

Don Swanson (*left*) and Jim Moore, both with USGS, view the car where photographer Reid Blackburn died. *USGS photo by Pete Lipman.*

Helens and Mount Margaret eight miles to the north. The eruption not only flattened millions of trees but also triggered some small forest fires. Then, the mountain smothered several fires it started with a blanket of heavy ash. Columns of ash boiled to a height of fifteen miles above the peak during a nine-hour period of emissions that day. The ash drifted east, turning day into night in towns in eastern Washington, northern Idaho and Montana and piling up several inches deep. Interstate 90, the major east–west route across the state, was in the middle of the ash storm and was closed for days from North Bend to the Montana border more than four hundred miles away.

A day later, Monday, May 19, a flow of hot volcanic ash and gases raced out of the now horseshoe-shaped mountain's crater and formed a two-hundred-foot mud-and-pumice dam at Spirit Lake. The new danger prompted rescue officials to evacuate more residents farther west of the mountain in the Toutle River Valley. Geologist Bob Christensen told me if the dam broke or overflowed, it would send a wall of water and debris down the river. The volcano spewed an emission of ash and steam to an elevation of eleven thousand feet above sea level. The ash was expected to reach Texas within a few days.

On Tuesday the twentieth, the mountain was relatively quiet, with eruptions limited to steam plumes. Earthquake activity had dropped dramatically. Visibility around the volcano was hampered by weather. Officials reported damage to trees in the timber-rich basins around the mountain was estimated to be about $200 million. Damage to other resources and facilities—roads, bridges, machinery, public water supplies and sanitation facilities, crops, wildlife and fisheries—climbed quickly past an incredible $500 million. Rail traffic in Washington and Oregon was halted or interrupted, and air travel in many parts of Washington had been rerouted or canceled. I felt fortunate to have grabbed a train to Vancouver the day of the eruption. All rail traffic between Seattle and Portland, including Amtrak passenger runs, was stopped because of fear that debris from the flooding Toutle River had weakened a rail bridge three miles north of Castle Rock. And I was here at the volcano center, ready for whatever happened next. That included, I learned, a visit by President Jimmy Carter, who was expected to tour the devastated areas, declare Washington State a disaster area and promise federal aid as soon as possible.

PRESIDENT CARTER AMAZED
AT VOLCANO'S DESTRUCTIVE POWER

When President Jimmy Carter inspected the devastated flanks of Mount St. Helens four days after the May 18, 1980 eruption, he was astonished at the sight.

"I cannot describe what I've seen here," Carter told scientists and media after the helicopter tour. "It is like nothing I have ever seen, or even heard about, in my life."

The small U.S. Marine Corps helicopter carrying President Carter got to within three miles of the volcano's summit before being turned back. Mount St. Helens, which was 9,677 feet high before it erupted, lost 1,300 feet when its top exploded northward and upward on that fateful Sunday morning.

Still, the president and his entourage were able to view much of the barren and ravaged landscape caused by the eruption and mudslides. Inclement weather prevented the president's helicopter from reaching the Spirit Lake area, where a dam had been formed by debris spewed from the mountain, creating behind it a lake of water, mud and ash. The flight, however, took Carter far enough along the Toutle River to see much of the devastation from pyroclastic flows and mudslides.

Several other helicopters followed behind the president's chopper carrying media, scientists and state emergency officials. Carter's entourage included Washington senator Warren G. Magnuson, Secretary of Interior Cecil Andrus and Robert Stevens, regional director of the Federal Emergency Management Agency.

At a news conference later in Portland, Oregon, President Carter said the devastation caused by the eruption exceeded his expectations, noting, "It's just an unbelievable sight, literally indescribable." He remarked that the ravaged terrain around Mount St. Helens was like a moonscape but added, "The moon looks like a golf course compared to what I've seen up there." He promised federal assistance wherever needed.

The previous day, the president was very attentive, I recall, to the information being presented at a briefing at the U.S. Geological Survey's Volcano Center in Vancouver, Washington, on the other side of the Columbia River. Carter met with Washington governor Dixy Lee Ray, scientists, U.S. Forest Service officials and local government leaders. More importantly, Carter signed Ray's request to declare Washington State a federal disaster area.

Carter, at the briefing, was astute about what was being discussed and entered into the conversation at the right moment. He urged that an inventory assessment be made to determine what tasks local, state and federal government could do. He informed everyone that Stevens was his representative to coordinate federal disaster relief efforts.

President Jimmy Carter (*in light coat third from left*) visited to see the devastation and talk to scientists. *Author's photo.*

At one point, Carter was listening to a report about the possible harvesting of downed timber lying on the ground like matchsticks from the enormous lateral blast of the volcano. Governor Ray interrupted the report presenter, stating, "The timber problem is down the road, Mr. President. There are people now unable to return to their homes and farmers who have experienced great loss. That's the top priority."

"What do you need?" Carter asked.

"M-O-N-E-Y," Ray replied, spelling out the word.

The president quipped that was why Magnuson was brought along. Magnuson was chairman of the Senate Appropriations Committee.

I heard Magnuson say he believed there was some emergency funding available, but he asked Governor Ray if the state was able to pay its share.

"We're paying our way now," Ray retorted. "What we need is some immediate cash."

President Carter said he envisioned a decades-long, expensive cleanup effort, adding that the trip demonstrated to him that a great deal of cooperation was needed from federal, state and local agencies to restore the area.

"The area can never be restored the way it was, but at least it can be made safe and habitable for people again," the president said.

Immediate concern centered on the Columbia River, inundated by mud and debris from Mount St. Helens. General Richard Wells of the Pacific Northwest Region of the U.S. Army Corps of Engineers told Carter the river would need to be dredged. He reported a number of large ships had been stranded in the clogged river channel. The depth was less than twenty-five feet and as little as twelve feet in some places. Wells said the plan was to use dredges to restore the river, within five months, to its normal six hundred feet wide and forty feet deep.

"What will be done with the spoil?" Carter asked.

Wells said the dredged material would be put on islands and on shores where it would have the least environmental impact.

President Carter said the mountain would have to continue to be monitored, and he offered his cabinet scientific adviser, Dr. Frank Press, to work with the state.

What did the future hold? Carter said he envisioned a time when Mount St. Helens could become a tourist attraction "to rival the Grand Canyon."

FORMER PRESIDENT CARTER PERMITS USE OF HIS DIARY ENTRY OF VISIT TO MOUNT ST. HELENS

Former president Jimmy Carter has been asked numerous times over the past two decades to participate in anniversary celebrations of the Mount St. Helens eruption of May 18, 1980, or to write something for volcano books, but he has declined. Until now. Carter agreed to be part of my book. In February 2019, I wrote a letter to former president Carter in Plains, Georgia, asking if he would write something about his remembrances of the day he visited the disaster zone. I heard back a month and a half later. He gave me permission to use his personal diary entry for May 22. That was the day after he attended a briefing by scientists and Washington governor Dixy Lee Ray in Vancouver, Washington.

When President Carter visited Mount St. Helens to see the devastation, he wasn't about to alter his daily exercise regimen. I watched him leave his hotel in Portland, Oregon, on the other side of the Columbia River. Carter was wearing jogging shorts and a T-shirt at 5:30 a.m. Secret service agents, in suits and ties, kept pace with him. He mentions that in his diary entry, which follows in its entirety:

> *Thursday, May 22, 1980*. In the morning, about 5:30, we ran 3 miles or so. And then took helicopters. Went down the Columbia River to the Kelso area where the Toutle and Cowlitz Rivers dump into the Columbia. The surge of ash carried by the rivers had clogged up the Columbia ship channel from a depth of 40 feet down to only 12 feet. We are moving

hopper dredges in there as quickly as possible to get the channel opened up because a number of ships are trapped in the Portland harbor and need to get a load of cargo out.

We then went up to Toutle Valley in the helicopter—first seeing large quantities of white-looking ash. And in the narrow river valley, we eventually began to see where the blast had directly burned the trees. Fifteen miles from the volcano, the trees had been burnt instantaneously with power at least equivalent to a 10-megaton nuclear explosion. The blast that followed in a few minutes had leveled every tree in an area of 150 square miles. One cubic mile off the side of the mountain had been pulverized, most of it into ash the consistency of face powder. Less than one micron in particle size. This ash had flowed down the mountain, carrying large chunks of ice, and also large rocks and molten lava.

Spirit Lake, the head of the Toutle River, was filled with 400 feet of ash and lava. The level of it had been raised 150 to 200 feet. And there was a dam 12 miles long below the lake.

This is nothing like I had ever seen. It was much worse than any photographs of the face of the moon. It looked like a boiling cauldron, because large icebergs the size of houses from the glaciers on the mountain were buried underneath hot ash and lava. The icebergs were melting and the surface of the ash was caving in.

The steam from the melting ice was rising. There were a few fires visible, but there was nothing much left to burn.

Eighty-five or 90 people were either dead or missing, including, unfortunately, some geologists who were handling the seismograph stations and instruments to assess the mountain's volcanic activity before it erupted.

The top 1,200 feet of the mountain was missing.

We couldn't get all the way to the mountain because of heavy steam and cloud formations. When the helicopter pilot decided to turn around, he didn't get any argument from me.

After a press conference [in Portland], *we went to Spokane. Although they only had about a half-inch deposit of ash, being 250 miles away, their airport was closed* [it remained so for twenty-two days] *because this extremely fine powder couldn't be controlled and was suspended in the air.*

At other places around Yakima and Ritzville the ash was as deep as 4 or 5 inches, and they're still not able to shovel their way out through this fine powder which has a specific gravity of about 2.7. It is non-toxic, and will ultimately be incorporated into the soil or on the bottom of lakes and streams, or carried out to sea.

Frank Press [Carter's science advisor] *says this is by far the biggest natural explosion ever recorded in North America in the last 4,000 years.*

Only because the volcano was very closely monitored, was the loss of life restricted. And, of course, it is in an isolated area, as well.

My inclination is not to clean up anything we don't have to, that's not directly affecting human life, but to let nature take its course in the valley region and around the mountain, which has a completely different geological configuration now.

TWO ATTACHED TO *NATIONAL GEOGRAPHIC* SAVED BY DINNER WHIM

A photographer and his assistant, both attached to *National Geographic*, who left their observation post near Mount St. Helens were "mad as hell" when they learned the volcano had erupted on Sunday, May 18, 1980. Kerry Webster, my colleague at the *Tacoma News Tribune*, reported the story during an interview with the two men. "After weeks of waiting patiently in the snow, we missed it," recounted freelance photographer Fred Stocker, who, with his assistant Jim McWhirter, left their tent camp the night before "on a whim to have dinner in town." McWhirter added, "We were furious because all we knew was that something big had happened and we missed it."

The two were shaken to learn later that the lateral blast had leveled their camp, leaving no sign of photographer Reid Blackburn of the Vancouver *Columbian*, whom they had left behind. It was mere chance, the roll of the dice, that Stocker and McWhirter weren't there. "We just decided to go down the mountain to have a nice dinner. No reason. It was totally spontaneous," said McWhirter. And then Stocker and McWhirter stayed overnight at a friend's place, intending to return the next day to the ridge where they had been stationed.

Stocker, McWhirter and Blackburn were part of a joint *Columbian-Geographic*-USGS effort to photograph volcanic activity on the bulging north flank of the steaming mountain. Their camp, Coldwater I, was on a ridge about eight miles from Mount St. Helens. Geologist David Johnston was in a trailer house at Coldwater II, a ridge three miles closer to the volcano, and was presumed killed in the blast, his body never recovered. "We thought that what we'd be seeing would be mudflows, and that everything would go into the valley below us and there would be no danger to ourselves," said Stocker. The lateral blast took everyone by surprise, blowing out everything in its path. "We had no idea the camp would take the full force of the explosion," Stocker said.

A helicopter pilot who flew over Coldwater I shortly after the blast reported no sign of life. The tent was gone, the ground was littered with fragments and Blackburn's Volvo sedan was skewed sideways, its windows blown out and ceiling upholstering hanging outside in strips. Days later, when rescue teams could get in on the ground, Blackburn was discovered dead in his car, the inside of which was filled with ash. "We were sorry about Reid and David," said Stocker, "but we knew how enthusiastic they were about what they were doing, and we knew we'd have been there, too, if things had been different." Fate intervened on behalf of Stocker and McWhirter. While Coldwater I was in operation, the two men were treated to fascinating close-ups of an evolving reawakened volcano. "We could see the bulge grow on the north side of the mountain," Stocker reflected. "We were taking time-lapse shots and developing them every day to see the difference."

Some evenings during their two-week vigil at Coldwater I, one or two of the group would drive the four or five miles down to the lodge at Spirit Lake operated by the eccentric Harry Truman, who was adamant to the last that the volcano wouldn't do anything. His lodge was closer than anything or anyone to the mountain. "We'd sit around and play his player piano," Stocker told Webster. "Harry was a great entertainer. We had a radio scanner and used to listen to David or the other USGS guys checking in with their base. It gave us a great sense of camaraderie to know there were others up there with us."

Stocker spent the night occasionally at the lodge, and one time, according to Truman's niece Shirley Rosen, a Redmond, Washington resident, Stocker and Truman experienced earthquakes that rumbled the lodge, shaking them and things hanging on walls. Despite a break from the task of monitoring the volcano, the earthquakes were a bit of a reminder of the imminent danger. As McWhirter noted, "We were aware we were in a hazardous area, of course, but we never really thought about it. The assumption was always that the blast would go up and the mudflow would go down."

However, the last few days before the big blast, Stocker opined, that feeling was beginning to change. "The thought started to occur to us that, with all that bulging and steaming, something was going to have to give." And he added, "I think David was the first to show signs of apprehension. He always said he was afraid of St. Helens, even though he couldn't bring himself to leave it." David Johnston figured that the continual building of the bulge on the north slope with little release of the pressure was going to result in something spectacular. He was right.

A TALE OF TERRIFYING SURVIVAL
THAT LIVES ON FOUR DECADES LATER

Tacomans Roald Reitan Jr. and Venus Dergan will never forget their harrowing experience being carried down the south fork of the Toutle River after Mount St. Helens erupted on May 18, 1980, when they were nineteen and twenty years old, respectively. Forty years have gone by, but their lives will be forever entwined. They were a couple in love at the time; they never married each other afterward but have remained friends. Their survival was miraculous to say the least. Waking up on Sunday, in the middle of a quiet fishing weekend thirty miles west of the mountain, they sensed something wasn't right. They couldn't see the peak from their campsite, but looking outside their tent, they saw a wall of water carrying logs and the remains of a wooden railroad trestle down the river toward their camp.

The couple moved quickly, grabbed their tent and chairs and shoved them in the trunk of Reitan's 1968 Oldsmobile. He tried to start the car, but it wouldn't turn over. Water was rapidly surrounding the car. "Get on the roof!" he shouted. They did, but water rose to their waists as the car began to tilt and float in the chocolate-brown muddy liquid. De-limbed logs from the Weyerhaeuser Company logging camp upstream crashed into the car.

With another huge log headed straight for them, Reitan yelled, "Jump!" and the couple leaped onto the rampaging logs and debris flow just seconds before the log smashed into the vehicle, overturning it into the muck. Reitan landed on a log. Dergan missed and wound up between his log and another. She disappeared from view. He yelled for her to "hang on" while saddled on a bull of a log that was taking him for a ride. A nearby log banged his knee. A couple of logs hit his back, sending stabs of pain through his body. Rising to his knees, Reitan crawled to the end of the log he was on and saw Dergan floating. He reached for her shirt and grabbed it but lost his grip, losing her to the muddy, swirling flow. Scrambling to a bigger log, he spotted her floating between two adjacent logs, jumped to the closest one and stretched down to grasp her. Grabbing her hair, he pulled like crazy. She was halfway out before she slipped from his arms and went back down and under as the two logs crashed together. "I'm sorry!" Reitan screamed. Dergan remembers trying to raise up her arm. When the logs finally separated, Reitan saw her uplifted arm, grabbed her wrist and pulled. He got her all the way out and secured her with his other arm so he wouldn't lose her. Reitan held Dergan close so they wouldn't both fall in. He was not going to let her go, clenching as tightly as he could.

With logs pushing them around, they floated into an area that Reitan recognized as a park. He figured here was their chance. The mudflow was slowing as the river channel widened. He instructed Dergan to follow him, jumping from log to log until they got close to shore, where they would need to make a big leap into the flow and hope it wasn't too deep. That's exactly what they did. The last leap of faith found them in muck up to their chests, but they were able to wade to shore. They made their way up a steep slope on all fours, using hands and feet to pull their way through thick brush and trees. Once on level, higher ground, Reitan assessed their injuries. He was battered, bruised and cut; a deep wound on his knee was trickling blood. Dergan's face, caked with thick mud, was oozing blood from wounds inflicted by logs that had hit her. An open gash extended from her wrist to her elbow, and she could see bone underneath. She felt her wrist was broken. Both had bloody, scraped feet. They hadn't had time to put on shoes when leaving their camp. How had they made it this far on bare feet?

Suddenly, they heard the noise of a plane and helicopter above them and began shouting. They realized trees were preventing anyone from seeing them. So they ran farther to a bridge, where they spotted a sheriff's vehicle, a deputy and two other men. They were safe. Later, they were helicoptered out to a hospital. I remember interviewing them in the hospital and writing a story. Other newspapermen and TV crews followed suit.

Over the years, at various anniversaries of the St. Helens eruptions, the media focused on Reitan and Dergan to retell their tale of survival. They have done so for newspapers, they've been the subject of documentaries and have been whisked to New York City to appear on network TV shows. Has it been too much for them? Have they tired of the periodic attention throughout their lives? They've tolerated it because they realized it happened to them together, and thus, they both needed to tell the story together, even if it was again and again. While they're grateful they survived, they cannot forget something so dramatic in their lives, though they've tried to put the experience in the rear-view mirror and move on.

Venus Dergan said, when I contacted her for an update for this book, that she and Reitan appeared in a Smithsonian Institution–produced film several years ago because she respects everything about the Smithsonian, but she was still pondering whether to accept a recent invitation from *National Geographic*. She was uncertain whether Reitan had been contacted or if he would go for it either.

Over the past forty years, she said, she has worked in a number of jobs and volunteered in the south Tacoma community. She worked as a travel agent, went around the world in that capacity and was in a couple of relationships that didn't work out. Reitan was married and had a child, Roald Reitan III, but the marriage didn't last, Dergan said. Later, she and Reitan rekindled their love and lived together, but eventually they went their separate ways.

When the 9-11 terrorist attack occurred in New York City, the travel industry was negatively impacted, and she knew she needed to find another livelihood. "I got a job in the healthcare business helping active military veterans and found it rewarding," Dergan said. She moved on later to her current job with a company that contracts directly with the federal government to help all veterans—active and retired—especially those having difficulties getting Veterans Administration benefits.

Dergan is not taking for granted any minutes in her life, giving it all. She has volunteered for the Humane Society, becoming one of its strongest advocates. "I've rattled a few cages on behalf of the animal adoption program and made a lot of money for the Humane Society," she said, adding that her efforts were featured in a *Tacoma News Tribune* article. "I'm a quiet force, but I work hard to give back," she insisted, noting her involvement in the south Tacoma neighborhood council. Has she been effective? Let's just allow her comment to stand for itself: "The City of Tacoma knows me."

Surviving the Mount St. Helens eruption has given her strength to face anything life might throw her way, including cancer five years ago. Dergan has met other cancer survivors, and that has been as meaningful to her as meeting other survivors of the Mount St. Helens eruption.

Reitan has managed to survive, too, working various jobs, currently construction, and being part of a few revival efforts with Dergan to recount their volcano experience. But he is more reluctant to talk about it these days and is trying hard to put the volcano survival experience behind him.

COLLEAGUE NOTED SACRIFICE OF HAM RADIO OPERATOR REPORTING ERUPTION

Kerry Webster, a fellow reporter and outstanding writer, was an integral piece of the incredible team coverage by the *Tacoma News Tribune* of the Mount St. Helens eruption in 1980. He focused on the impact on Washington citizens living in the vicinity of the awesome volcano. A ham radio operator, Webster was empathetic to the work of one ham radio operator who sacrificed his life in giving the first heads up that the mountain was exploding on May 18. He remembers vividly the story he wrote about Gerald Martin, whose handle was W6TQF.

Martin, a retired navy veteran who originally hailed from Washington State, settled in California after leaving the service but frequently traveled in his motor home, volunteering to help in emergencies. The day of the eruption, he was positioned on a ridge facing the north slope of Mount St. Helens. For more than a month, his calm, accurate reports on 146.06 MHz, the Department of Emergency Services "volcano net" frequency, had helped state officials monitor the mountain's ash-and-steam outbursts. Martin's regular morning calls were as routine as morning coffee to Reade Apgar, a ham radio operator in Olympia, receiving Martin's reports. Mostly the reports had been similar conversation: "N7AGG, this is W6TQF. Good morning, Reade. It's a beautiful day up here. The mountain is clear, and there is no sign of activity."

However, on Sunday, May 18, Martin's thirty-second day, the normal chatting and observation of the weather suddenly took a terrifying turn. Apgar told Webster that W6TQF exclaimed, "Oh my gosh, would you look at that!" It was 8:32 a.m., and the top and north face of Mount St. Helens had just blown off. Remarkably, Martin remained on the air, relaying a graphic description of the black, boiling cloud of ash and steam that was racing toward him. Methodically, Martin switched to a second, longer-range radio to alert a statewide network of the eruption. Al Kinder, K7KNZ, acknowledged the message and heard Martin reply, "Now I've got to try to get the hell out of here." To Apgar, W6TQF made one last transmission: "Reade, you wouldn't believe this." Then, silence. "W6TQF, W6TQF, this is N7AGG. Are you okay, Gerry?" There was no answer.

Meanwhile, Webster reported, on the west side of the mountain Ty and Mary Ann Kearney, another ham radio couple, looked back as they fled in their own motor home. They noticed that the ridge where W6TQF had been was enveloped in thick, churning ash. Several days after the eruption, Kinder reported, a helicopter search "could not find even a piece of Martin's motor home." Kinder, a longtime acquaintance of Martin's, said his friend didn't have to be up on that ridge. "He was a volunteer, just an ordinary guy who wanted to help out."

Kinder noted that earlier in the spring of 1980, Martin had helped Los Angeles–area hams with communications during serious flooding in Southern California. "Gerry's value to a communications net was that he never got excited, never exaggerated and never reported anything he couldn't see or confirm for himself," Kinder said. State officials declared that Martin's timely warning, coming literally at the moment of the eruption, helped agencies gain precious minutes of lead time in organizing rescue missions. "When the mountain blew, Gerry got the message out first and worried about himself second," said Kinder. "That was the mark of a real pro."

MOUNT ST. HELENS' SECOND MAJOR ERUPTION BLEW ASH DIFFERENTLY

While most people were just waking up for the Sunday, May 18, 1980 eruption at 8:32 a.m., they were likely asleep when the second major eruption occurred on Sunday, May 25, at 2:30 a.m., spreading a plume of smoke and ash as high as forty thousand feet. Spotter planes and weather radar tracked the black cloud as a southeasterly wind carried it over Cowlitz, Lewis, Thurston, Mason, Grays Harbor and Clallam Counties. That was opposite of normal prevailing westerly and southwesterly winds, which carried ash the week before to eastern Washington and beyond, including Montana and the central part of the United States. Newspaper colleague Kerry Webster was there to report much of the activity.

Meanwhile, scientists were observing this activity that included at least one pyroclastic flow and small to moderate ash falls in communities spared the ash fall of May 18.

Ash from the second explosion created distinct differences depending on where people were living. There was no dawn in the town of Castle Rock as the ash-darkened sky rained mud and flashed dim red lightning through the volcanic gloom. The ash, mixed with a drizzling rain, fell in gritty globules that spattered when they hit. Streets were covered with the glop in minutes, and windshield wipers quickly became useless. In Longview, Kelso and Castle Rock, power went out as the wet, conductive ash shorted out insulators and transformers. Dull booms echoed in the unnatural darkness as electrical equipment exploded. "This is just incredible," said teenager Jeff Johnston, muffled in a painter's mask as he walked the deserted streets of Castle Rock in search of flashlight batteries. "I can't believe this stuff. It's everywhere." Because of its location west of the mountain, Castle Rock received the heaviest ashfall in Cowlitz County—just over a quarter of an inch in about five hours. "I was sure hoping we could get by without the dang ash," said Castle Rock mayor Mike Huson, surveying the glop on his sidewalk. "It's not as if we didn't have enough trouble already, what with the mud and flooding from May 18."

Quick-thinking truckers who formed moving roadblocks with their rigs were credited with keeping Interstate 5 open during the night as clouds of volcanic ash whirled about prior to late-arriving rain. State troopers said truckers, hailing one another on CB radio, began driving their rigs three abreast at twenty-five miles per hour, forcing car drivers behind them to do the same. "Immediately, the accident rate dropped and the dust began to clear," reported State Patrol sergeant C.W. Elder. An emergency twenty-five-mile-per-hour speed limit had been imposed but was virtually ignored by impatient drivers. Elder said he saw cars going as fast as seventy miles per hour in the passing lane, kicking up ash dust and spreading clouds over both sides of the freeway. "Sometimes it was so thick, I couldn't see the end of my own hood," Elder exclaimed.

After a multicar accident blocked northbound lanes at the Spirit Lake cutoff for more than an hour, "the truckers got mad and took matters into their own hands," the sergeant reported. Waving CB microphones and blowing airhorns, the truckers jockeyed their rigs into position across all three lanes of the freeway and slowed to twenty-five miles per hour as angry, honking motorists piled up behind. The three-truck platoons were spaced out at intervals of about seven miles, Elder noted, or just enough space for the dust to settle before the next bunch came along. The State Patrol district office in Kelso logged hundreds of calls from irate travelers, but they were told blandly that the truckers were acting on their own. "Of course, we don't condone what the truckers did," said Sergeant Elder, with a snickering sound. "But it sure as hell saved a lot of lives, and it kept the freeway open." A slight rain later left freeway conditions somewhat improved, but blowing ash was still common south of Castle Rock toward the town of Kalama.

A battered old Chevrolet bus, laden with roped-on bicycles and plastered with "No Nuke" stickers, groaned into the gas station in the town of Toledo, twenty miles north of Castle Rock, under a thick layer of ash. Its occupants turned out to be a group of young protesters from California on their way to the Trident nuclear submarine base at Bangor, Washington, on the Olympic Peninsula. "Right now we're more interested in survival than protest, to tell you the truth," said the shaken driver, Toby Grant. "This kind of fallout is almost as scary as the nuclear kind." Tourist Joy Rodden of Chillicothe, Illinois, said she didn't know about the ash cloud when she woke up in the dark. "I looked at the clock, turned to my husband and said, 'I don't think I'd like to live out here, look how late the sun comes up in the morning.'"

To the southwest of Mount St. Helens, in Cougar, the soft patter of rain was almost the only sound on Sunday, May 25, as mist rolling off the foothills of the volcano engulfed the town. A metal sign squeaked in the wind at the closed Shell gas station, and a lone raven croaked overhead. Water droplets plunked monotonously onto the canvas of a stored snowmobile. Some residents, who left in the wake of the early morning eruption, were returning as evening approached. Others never had left. "No, I couldn't see any sense in it," said Dot Elmire, who was still at her cash register in the Cougar Store. "This is something we're going to have to live with for a long time. We can't pick up and run every time the mountain blows a little ash on us."

Cougar, then a community of about 250 full-time residents, is about eight miles south of the volcano at the edge of Yale Lake. It was officially evacuated twice—once on May 18 and again on May 25. Elmire stayed put both times. So did about two dozen others. When the mountain blew on May 18, she reported that people "could look up and see the cloud as it came right over the store, mushrooming just like an atomic bomb. It wasn't fluffy like a cloud, though. It looked thick and heavy." The Cougar Store's few customers on May 25 were either local holdouts or newspersons, since rifle-wielding National Guardsmen turned everybody else back at Yale, about five miles west on Highway 503. She was pleased that her plastic-wrapped packages of "genuine volcanic ash" were selling well at $1.81 for about a tablespoon-full.

The Cougar Store phone was ringing off the hook as townspeople called to see whether it was safe to return. "I'm telling them, 'Heck yes, c'mon home,'" laughed Elmire. In the Lone Fir Resort, which also houses the town liquor store, Earl and Jimmie Barcus and their partners, Don and Marilyn Platt, had just returned. "Want to buy a nice motel?" Mrs. Barcus joked, gesturing toward a row of unused room keys on pegs. Earl Barcus said he wasn't particularly nervous about coming back, believing the mountain had "shot its wad" on the north side. But, he added cautiously, "now if there was a new bulge growing on the south side, like there was on the north side just before the eruption, you can bet we'd hightail it out of here. We're the same distance from the mountain as all the people who got killed on the other side." But partner Don Platt said he figured pressure had been released and that "the mountain probably has done all she's gonna do, except maybe some more ash." The motel's CB radio crackled. It was another resident, Ron Katzer, returning to his shuttered A&R Grocery up the street. "Well, we're back," Katzer said. "Doesn't look too bad, except for some ash on the ground." "Welcome back, Trailblazer," replied Platt, using Katzer's CB handle. "Just wait'll you start tracking that stuff inside." "Hi, Don, we'll be down to your place in a minute," the radio crackled back. "I think we're outta whiskey."

Back at the Cougar Store, Elmire was sweeping ash off the antler-draped front porch. A couple of meadowlarks chirped on the single telephone wire, and a bright yellow goldfinch picked at crumbs in the gravel. "I like it when it's quiet like this," she said. "This is probably the quietest this town has been since back in March, when the mountain started doing things." Pausing a moment to gather her thoughts, she reflected, "You know, it's amazing how much the mountain has changed our lives. All of a sudden, this beautiful mountain that you looked upon as a serene, wonderful thing has changed into—well, something entirely different. And I guess we'll just have to get used to it, won't we?" Two weeks after this activity, the mountain erupted

A lava dome began rising on the floor of the horseshoe-shaped crater. *Author's photo.*

The dome kept growing for months after the May 18 eruption. *Author's photo.*

Geologists gathered samples by hand from vents on the dome and crater during a post-eruptive period in 1980. *USGS photo by Thomas Casadevall.*

Steam poured out of the crater as the lava dome built layer upon layer. *Author's photo.*

The mountain had a layer of fresh snow during its first winter after eruptions. *Author's photo.*

again on June 12, again depositing ash to the south and southwest, hitting Cougar with another dusting and answering Elmire's question about having to become accustomed to the volcano's interruptions in their lives.

Within hours of the latest eruption, but hidden by poor visibility around the peak, scientists surmised that stiff magma had begun to ascend in the crater vent, slowly oozing onto the crater floor and forming a bulbous lava dome that became 1,200 feet in diameter and 150 feet high. They eventually confirmed this formation, which became the first of three domes at Mount St. Helens during 1980. A July 22 explosive eruption destroyed the June lava dome. No dome developed then. Explosive episodes on August 7 were followed by the formation of a small dome, but that was blasted away during activity between October 16 and 18, the last major explosive period of 1980. Subsequently, another dome began to form almost immediately and within a few days had grown to 900 feet wide and 130 feet high. In between episodes, scientists would sample gases in the crater. Eruptive episodes continued throughout the decade, and by the start of 1990, a composite dome was about 3,480 feet by 2,820 feet in diameter and rose about 1,150 feet above the crater floor. Scientists predicted it would take more than two hundred years, at a calculated rate of 17 million cubic yards a year, to rebuild Mount St. Helens to its pre-1980 size.

THOSE ESCAPING ST. HELENS BLAST
DESCRIBED DEVASTATION

When my fellow *Tacoma News Tribune* reporter Kerry Webster talked to folks escaping the awesome devastation of the Mount St. Helens explosion on May 18, 1980, he saw fatigue on their ash-covered faces. He still remembers vividly the experience today, telling me he also sensed the relief that these volcano refugees felt in making it to one of several shelters set up in Kelso, Washington, about forty miles west of the mountain. As they trickled in twos and threes into shelters, Webster asked them for their stories.

Pat Kilgore, a logger living along the Toutle River, said, "The mud just swept everything away. I saw log trucks, dump trucks and cars overturned and buried in mud." Jeannette Squires, who fled Silver Lake with her children, said, "Whole houses and mobile homes were coming down the river along with the logs and mud." Another logger, Randy Peck, told of helping to rescue two young campers, a man and a woman, whose tent had been swept away by a mudflow. "They told me they heard a rumble and unzipped the tent flap just in time to see a wall of mud coming right at them. It picked up their tent, their car, everything. The girl was pinned under a log with a broken leg and arm. My brother-in-law and I had to wade through mud up to our chests to get to them."

Kilgore, Squires and Peck were among about twenty people from the Toutle River Valley who found beds in a Red Cross shelter set up in a junior high school. Most had been plucked from their riverside homes by helicopter. Grant Christensen was covered from head to toe with fine white ash as he munched a lukewarm hamburger in the school gym. A little terrier dog sat at his feet. "Me and my brother were going to get his tools out of Camp Baker, where he works, but the ash was so heavy it got into the motor of the pickup, and she choked up and wouldn't go no more," he explained. "I guess we walked fourteen, fifteen miles before the chopper picked us up. And if I walked fifteen miles, old Rusty here"—he scratched the dog's ears—"he musta walked a hundred." Christensen contemplated his hamburger ruefully. "So, now, I've lost my truck and my tools as well. We didn't gain much out of that trip, I'm afraid."

Vera Mae Gardner, the Toutle River mail carrier, said she and her husband were sitting down to breakfast "when there was this huge rumble outside. I thought it was a train. But my husband said, 'No, by God, it's the river!' So we ran for the hill behind our house. We have seventy head of cattle, and they ran right along with us." Teenager Shelly Winningham said it was neat when things started, "but all of a sudden it got dark with this huge cloud from the mountain. There was red lightning. After that, it got pretty scary." Randy Peck watched the first mudflow pass as he stood at Harry Gardner Park on the Toutle River and "just couldn't believe my eyes." He said the mud had "settled down into a big plateau, like one giant mud pie, that must have been half a mile wide. There were mud marks thirty feet up the few trees left standing. It was amazing. I just stared at it."

Although the Red Cross was prepared to handle several thousand volcano refugees, only a few dozen showed up at shelters. Nolan Lewis, Cowlitz County emergency services director, said most of the people figured Mount St. Helens was going to do something big and had "made arrangements to stay with relatives." He noted that "people around here are pretty self-reliant." Lewis said that most of the two hundred residents of Cougar had evacuated, as had almost everyone in the town of Toutle. And the residents were anxious to return to their homes, if anything was left. Pat Kilgore said he was ready to return, once authorities let them, despite the danger. "You bet I'm going back," said Kilgore. "I've already got firewood stacked for the winter."

AL MILLIKEN CASHED IN ON ASH LIKE NO ENTREPRENEUR

Longview resident Al Milliken was quicker than most when it came to entrepreneurship in the wake of the Mount St. Helens disaster. He had a plan for taking advantage of the twist in wind patterns that dumped ash on his sidewalk and driveway after the volcano's explosion on May 25, 1980. He decided he would sell volcanic ash in a clear ballpoint pen. That meant that Milliken; his wife, Jeannine; and two of their three children spent all day sweeping up the ash. And finding a place to store it. In Milliken's way of thinking, he was "killing two birds with one stone"—cleaning up ash at his home while launching an endeavor he hoped would help him clean up in another way. That big way was possibly making some money from his idea. He told the *Longview Daily News* he had formed a company, Al Milliken Mount St. Helens Volcanic Ash Ballpoint Pen Co., to market his product.

A.J. Milliken, a manager for Conifer Foods, which sells the famous Fisher Scones in Washington State, remembers his father's financial venture, but first he felt it was important to note that "my dad was a junior and I'm a third." In fact, some of his friends and fellow employees call him "Albert." To my son Keith and me, he is A.J. We often work with him to make, bake and sell Fisher Scones. A.J. was one of the children who shoveled and swept the ash. "When we got done sifting it, we had two hundred pounds of ash," A.J. recounted. "My father ordered one thousand pen casings and was awaiting delivery from New York." At the time, Milliken told the Longview newspaper that he "only started with a thousand to see how that would work," adding, "I haven't very much money, I'm not a rich man." A Weyerhaeuser employee,

Milliken was renowned for his car racing prowess, winning often at various tracks throughout western Washington. A.J. has memories of working in the pits at the racetracks, to the envy of all his school chums. He's not surprised about his dad's ash-in-pens effort, knowing how innovative his father was when it came to boosting the performance of his Chevy racing cars.

A.J.'s father got the idea from pens that banks gave out with shredded dollar bills in them. "Selling ash in little bags or in bottles is kind of boring," his dad said. "You put ash in a pen and people can take it with them wherever they go and show it off." A genuine keepsake, the pens had "Authentic volcanic ash—Mount St. Helens 1980" stamped on them. A plug holding the ash in each pen came off so the owner could pour the grit out for closer inspection. But Milliken sold no ash refills, noting each was a "one-time shot."

A.J. recalls that his dad sold ten thousand pens at "a dollar or dollar and a half" apiece; he cannot remember for sure the exact price. Two retail outlets in Longview—Handy Andy's and Bob's Surplus—were the main locations selling his father's pens. Milliken made his mark, so to speak. You could say he had the "write" stuff.

DAVID JOHNSTON KNEW
MOUNT ST. HELENS WAS DANGEROUS

My fellow newspaper reporter Kerry Webster described the pre–May 18 eruption situation at Timberline below the north flank of Mount St. Helens. He told me it was a bizarre scene, too frightening to be funny, too comic to be drama. Looking up toward the volcano's slope threatening to erupt, a young scientist was explaining to half a dozen shivering reporters, bracing against a cold wind, how we could all be killed at any moment. "It's like we're standing on a powder keg and the fuse has been lit, but we don't know how long it is," said volcanologist David Johnston. "This is an extremely dangerous place to be."

A week or so after Webster's encounter with Johnston, I remember being at the same place and getting the same warning from Johnston. Webster's memories resonate with me even today, in 2020. Webster said Johnston, with one wary eye on the mountain, was urging reporters to get out of the area as soon as possible. He warned that the mountain's north slope was building up pressure, creating a bulge that was growing day by day. The reporters kept asking questions, so fascinated by what Johnston was saying that they just couldn't leave Timberline.

"I'm not going to stick around any longer than necessary," Johnston said. "Why?" asked a reporter. "Because," the scientist explained patiently, "an eruption could send an avalanche of red-hot magma, traveling at better than sixty miles per hour, directly at the spot where we are standing." "Oh," the reporter said weakly. Only moments earlier, Johnston had returned from a fly-over of the mountain in a U.S. Forest Service helicopter to examine the huge crater left by steam explosions during the reawakening phase that started in late March 1980.

Johnston said that a steam explosion is a common occurrence in the early stages of a volcanic eruption. It is caused, he explained, by the too-rapid release of pent-up moisture through heated rock. Termed "phreatic eruptions," they include emissions of steam, ash and volcanic rock. Throughout late March and April, phreatic eruptions were occurring with great regularity.

"If I was looking for the one single event which is most often the precursor of a magmatic eruption, I would choose a steam explosion," he said. "I'm not trying to be an alarmist, and I'm usually pretty calm around volcanoes, but I am genuinely afraid of this thing. I am leaving the mountain as soon as possible, and I urge you to do the same." The reporters pondered Johnston's message of imminent danger. Someone finally drew his attention to a plume of white vapor on the rim of the mountain. "Oh boy," Johnston reacted. "Is that cloud, or is it steam?" Before the sentence had ended, half a dozen news cars were in gear and racing down the mountain. Eight hours later, another explosion expanded the size of the crater on the volcano's summit.

Given the increasing seismic and volcanic activity, Johnston and other volcanologists working for the USGS in Vancouver prepared to observe the volcano for impending eruptions. They established Coldwater I and Coldwater II observation posts on ridges north of the mountain to use laser ranging to measure how the distances to reflectors installed close to the mountain changed over time. That helped them calculate how much the bulge on the volcano's north flank was growing.

From early May until May 10, phreatic eruptions were intermittent. On May 16 and 17, those types of eruptions ceased. But the bulge was still increasing. Something had to give. And it did. The north face of the mountain blew out on the morning of May 18 in a lateral avalanche that went outward for miles, killing Johnston. But his dedication to his job of taking part in the dangerous on-site monitoring helped warn people to stay away from the volcano and led to the public closure of the area around the peak. He felt that the greatest threat was from an eruption to the north originating from the bulge. He was right.

Johnston's colleagues praised him as a hardworking, enthusiastic and genuine individual who was already filled with so much experience in his young life and was loaded with potential for a bright future. Dr. Steve Malone, a seismologist who was Johnston's mentor at the University of

Washington, where Johnston earned his PhD in volcanology, reflected that the thirty-year-old scientist "was very good at his work" and died doing what he loved.

One of the first newsmen to reach Johnston's parents, Tom and Alice Johnston, in Illinois, I had to convince them that I was not like some from the media who badgered them with questions about their son's risk taking. I explained that I understood the need for taking risks and had done so myself on my job as a journalist covering Mount St. Helens and in my recreational climbs of Washington State mountains. They opened up to me, albeit briefly, as they were overcome with emotion and grief. But they did converse with me. They said they cherished his phone calls to them during his time on St. Helens and knew that he loved his work as a volcanologist. They said, "Not many people get to do what they really want to do in this world, but our son did."

The passionate scientist recognized for his heroic dedication to the field of volcanology and especially Mount St. Helens has been remembered with memorials honoring his life. One of the early acts of commemoration included two trees planted in Tel Aviv, Israel, and the renaming in his hometown of Oak Lawn, Illinois, of a facility as the David Johnston Community Center. Both happened during the first anniversary of the eruption in 1981. On the second anniversary, the USGS office in Vancouver was renamed the David A. Johnston Cascades Volcano Observatory. A memorial grove of trees in Cowlitz County, Washington, provides welcome repose over a plaque honoring the fifty-seven people, including Johnston, who died as a result of the 1980 St. Helens eruption. Two trees were planted on the grounds of the USGS office in Menlo Park, California, where Johnston had worked. Johnston's connections with the University of Washington are remembered by a memorial fund that established an endowed graduate-level fellowship called the David A. Johnston Memorial Fellowship for Research Excellence. Two other public memorials near Mount St. Helens include Johnston's name among those who died—one on a large curved granite memorial at a place that bears his name, the Johnston Ridge Observatory, and a second on a plaque at the Hoffstadt Bluffs Visitor Center.

AL EGGERS RECALLS GRAVITY MEASUREMENTS ON ST. HELENS AND KILAUEA

Former University of Puget Sound geology professor Al Eggers vividly remembers the day Mount St. Helens surprised him—March 27, 1980. Shrouded in clouds, the volcano was hidden from sight at the Timberline parking lot where Eggers and his team of student researchers had gathered to begin gravity measurements on the north flank of the mountain.

"I was walking along Spirit Lake," Eggers, retired, now living in Lewistown, Montana, said softly. "The snow was fifteen feet deep, and I suddenly heard a noise like sheet metal shaking. It scared the heck out of me." He'd heard that kind of noise before during a volcanic eruption, he told me recently. He quickly made his way to the lodge operated by Harry Truman to warn anyone there. He noticed a vehicle that hadn't been there earlier. It was a news team from the *Columbian*. He told them and Truman what he had heard and what he suspected had occurred on the mountain. An emission was confirmed later in the day by airplane flights during breaks in the clouds and visualized further three days later when clearer weather returned to the area.

UPS students constructed a dry-tilt station at Timberline to measure surface deformation and later made concurrent measurements of the lake water level using yard sticks, effectively using Spirit Lake as a tilt meter. Eggers remembers Truman as a character who acted like a magnet with regard to his students. "I had a problem with my students escaping and I couldn't find them," he said. "Then I went to Truman's lodge and found students being entertained with Truman serving them whiskey-

Coke drinks and showing them 8mm movies." One of his students, Dan Johnson, became particularly astute, winding up as a field assistant at Cascades Volcano Observatory in Vancouver and honing the skills of monitoring an active, dangerous volcano. After the May 18 eruption, particularly in 1981 and a few more years beyond that, Johnson installed the first tilt meters in the crater of St. Helens that helped predict a series of dome-building eruptions.

Eggers went on, as did Johnson, to work at Kilauea, one of the most active volcanoes in the world, gathering raw gravity measurements that were corrected for effects of earth tides, instrument drift and concurrent elevation changes. Their data showed that residual gravity had steadily increased in an area centered on the southeast rim of Halemaumau Crater. Of course, legend has it that the Hawaiian goddess of volcanoes, Pele, resides there, the hottest spot on the mountain. Eggers finished Johnson's twenty-six-year research on Kilauea after Johnson and a colleague were killed in October 2005 when their vehicle was involved in an accident with a logging truck that lost its load on Highway 101 near Humptulips. At a memorial at UPS, where Johnson was a professor, Eggers remembered Johnson as a "steady friend and dear man whose loss leaves large voids in the fabric of our lives and science."

Eggers took Johnson's data and maps and turned it into a report on "Residual Gravity Changes in Kilauea: 1977–2003," coauthored by the two scientists. He presented it to the American Geophysical Union at its fall meeting in 2006. As a result of the detailed study of Kilauea over a long period of time, a noteworthy finding is that there are void spaces—a network of interconnected cracks rather than a single large cavern—beneath the volcano's surface. Magma accumulation in these voids causes a gravity increase due to the addition of mass. Measurements have allowed volcanologists to detect rapid changes in mass beneath the surface that might otherwise go undetected. They have also revealed insights about a lava lake at Kilauea's summit. In recent years, the dropping of the lava lake level coincided with a major decrease in gravity measured by an instrument on the rim of Halemaumau. The lake has drained due to fissure eruptions near Puu Oo on the volcano's East Rift Zone, creating volcanic events that have caused anxiety for residents of the Big Island on a regular basis.

Eggers is proud to be part of that gravity research over the years and has been sharing stories with someone seeking to write a book about him. Both Mount St. Helens and Kilauea have become natural laboratories by which scientists can refine techniques, including gravity measurements, to study volcanoes. Eggers agrees somewhat that new monitoring tools have made it less likely that geologists such as David Johnston, who died during the big St. Helens eruption, will have to be positioned on ridges to observe activity. But he maintained, "Some measurements need to be done close up." And he has great admiration for Johnston. But there's always risks for scientists. "Johnston was no different in that regard than the rest of us," Eggers mused. "He was there [Coldwater II ridge] because no one else was there."

STRANGE LADY OF THE VOLCANO

A bit of weirdness came out during the months following the May 18, 1980 eruption of Mount St. Helens, with visions of a goddess who showed up and then vanished. The tale of her presence spread almost as fast as the ash from the volcano carried around the world.

One driver didn't know what to make of it when a young woman hitchhiker got into his car on Highway 12 near Morton, Washington, some eighty miles north of the volcano. She was strikingly beautiful with haunting eyes. He listened intently as she spoke, her conversation taking on a foreboding tone. She warned of an eruption between October 12 and 14, 1980, that would devastate an area within a hundred-mile radius of St. Helens. Her eyes seemed to pierce right through him. His eyes turned back to the road, and when they returned to the seat—she was gone.

Gone! He almost lost control of his car in his astonishment over what had happened.

He thought he must be losing his mind. He didn't know whether he should report the incident to authorities for fear of being considered crazy or drunk. But he had to tell someone, so he told friends. The story, as all such ones do, spread like the ash itself from the erupting volcano. And that's how I heard about it, word of mouth, and decided to check it out. The rumor of a vanishing lady making St. Helens predictions was going around. Some even went so far as to suggest she resembled Pele, the Hawaiian goddess of volcanoes.

Legend has it that Pele takes the form of a woman, young or old, with varying features or garb, and appears to offer warnings. Whoever encounters her must warn others or suffer misfortune during a subsequent eruption. While incidents involving Pele are usually confined to the Hawaiian islands, this was new ground.

A U.S. Forest Service spokeswoman told me that she had heard of the sightings but that the Forest Service had not received any direct reports, verbal or written. Rumors of the sightings, she noted, had been mostly centered near the mountain, particularly in the Morton-Randle-Packwood area. The reports of the warnings were consistent— of devastation between October 12 and 14 that would be greater than the explosive eruption of May 18, which destroyed the area north of St. Helens and killed fifty-seven people.

Robert Dunnagan, chief of operations at Mount Rainier National Park, answered my inquiry, saying he, too, had heard the reports of Pele sightings passed on by his park colleagues. But he questioned the comparison to Pele, telling me, "What does she look like? I don't think anyone knows. Shoot, I know about the warnings, too, but you've got me what to make of them. I'll really be impressed with the vanishing lady if something happens, though."

No agency—not the State Patrol, Cowlitz and Lewis County sheriff departments, the USGS or FEMA—received any direct report of the vanishing lady.

About the closest thing to an official report was a second-hand account to the City of Morton Police Department. "We received a rumor that some people picked up a lady with a white gown on," said Morton police chief Jim Endrud. "She gave her warning, and when they looked in the back seat, she was gone. And they were going sixty miles an hour down the road. But I don't know what they were smokin' or drinkin'."

The *Forks Forum* published a story about a Forks man who reported picking up a woman on a backroad in the Mount St. Helens area near the town of Randle and claimed that the woman disappeared after giving her warning. The newspaper, located on Washington's Olympic Peninsula near the Pacific Ocean, made mention of the woman's description matching the volcano goddess Pele.

But Chief Endrud said the tale "just got wilder and longer" as it was retold and passed along. There were also reports of loggers driving their timber-loaded logging trucks and picking up the mysterious lady. "It was all hearsay," Endrud said. "We had nothing to confirm it."

Later, the USGS scientists in the volcano center in Vancouver, Washington, reported that there was no major eruption between October 12 and 14, only "small seismic events and minor gas emissions at irregular intervals." So much for that prediction. However, the last major explosive activity of the 1980s occurred between October 16 and 18 with ash flows to forty-seven thousand feet and some pyroclastic flows. But it was nothing as catastrophic as the prediction.

PART IV

RECOVERY

BOTANISTS FOUND LIFE RETURNING TO MOUNT ST. HELENS

Two years after Mount St. Helens erupted with a bang heard around the world, A.B. Adams was on the devastated landscape trying to find signs of life. Lying prone on the debris flow, he pushed his face into a mud hole and exclaimed, "There's one. A willow seed!" To the casual observer, the mud hole was as devoid of life as the surrounding terrain, but to Adams, it was rich volcanic soil ready to spring back to life. "This is where life begins," he reflected. "If I were a seed, this is where I'd want to land."

A.B. and his wife, Virginia Adams, were engaged on a determined search for flora on the gray mudflow stretching down the north fork of the Toutle River and on the nearby timber-scarred ridges. With a master's degree in botany, he was attached to the University of Washington geophysics department. As a spokesman for that department, A.B. had kept the news media and general public informed about what Mount St. Helens was doing before the big blast. Virginia, with a doctorate in mathematical ecology, had taught at UW and at Pacific Lutheran University (PLU). They had the perfect background to head an effort dedicated to recording the volcano's rebirth. They had received funding from Earthwatch, a Massachusetts-based nonprofit organization, and were leading a team of volunteers who were part of the scientific research project. News photographer Bob Rudsit and I from the *Tacoma News Tribune* were covering the story.

A.B. and Virginia believed that all of the species of flora would eventually return to the mountain's landscape. Monitoring the debris plain for several months before launching the Earthwatch endeavor, they had

Virginia and A.B. Adams *(first two on the right)* directed the botany study. *Author's photo.*

already recorded about half of the total number of species. In particular abundance at that time was fireweed, which A.B. declared was "the hero of the devastation flow." Other species included thimbleberry, ragwort, miner's lettuce, rushes, willows and alpine lupine. The latter was really out of its habitat, generally found at higher elevations but moved to this lower spot by the mudflow.

"It's simply amazing," A.B. told me. "We could have the only alpine meadow in the world at three thousand feet."

The couple made good use of the volunteer team members. The volunteers set up seed traps. Each trap consisted of two stakes pounded in the ground, a piece of wood attached to the stakes on top and grease and oil–soaked cheesecloth spread across and stapled to the wood frame. The sticky cloth would catch and hold any windblown seeds that hit it. Using a compass, the team positioned the traps in a straight line fifty meters apart on the debris flow. Each trap was placed to take advantage of the prevailing winds, which happened to be from the southwest. Near each sticky trap, Virginia and the team dug two small holes twenty centimeters deep. "They simulate human or animal tracks," she explained. "Such depressions serve as traps for seeds because they retain more moisture than the surface." Dirt from the holes was piled up in equal-sized mounds. "The mounds," she said,

Fireweed was the hero of the natural recovery, returning faster than other plants. *USGS photo.*

Lupine growing on the devastated land might take one hundred years to flourish, as it did before the 1980 eruption. *Author's photo.*

Left: Traps were put in place, using burlap with a sticky substance, to capture seeds. *Author's photo*.

Below: A.B. bent over to get a better look at a seedling coming back. *Author's photo*.

Photographer Bob Rudsit was prone to get his close-up shot, as A.B. Adams pointed out evidence of plant life returning. *Author's photo.*

"simulate small animal lairs on which plant life is more apt to grow because the mounds hold more moisture."

A.B. followed behind to ascertain the numbers and types of plant species within an eight-meter radius of each test plot. That's how he wound up lying with his face in the mud. At that particular mud hole, he estimated there "were hundreds of willow seeds waiting for a good rain" to germinate. He predicted a "virtual oasis" by summer's end. Closer examination revealed to him possible thistle, blueberry and black cottonwood plants.

The team spent several days placing seed traps in other locations, including on the slopes above Castle Lake a few miles away from the debris flow close to the horseshoe-shaped crater. A.B. and Virginia identified species there that included rushes, sedges, vanilla leaf (*Achlys triphylla*), blueberry, inside-out flower (*Vancouveria hexandra*), elderberry and a dogwood herb (*Cornus canadensis*). There also was *Trillium ovatum*, a member of the lily family. Identification of that drew a note of optimism from A.B.: "If trillium, which is very delicate, can make it, anything will."

Not like other researchers, A.B. and Virginia took exception to those scientists who declared the land had been obliterated. A.B. explained that some scientists were so busy studying the volcanic activity of the mountain after it erupted that they didn't bother to consult any botanists. "They looked at the land and assumed everything had been destroyed," he said. "They considered the eruption an unusual occurrence." Maybe to man it was, A.B. explained, but not to plants. To the plants, he maintained, the eruption was probably no different than a devastating fire. Scientists could have drawn from research conducted on other volcanoes in Alaska, Japan and the Soviet Union to find out how plants come back. The Adamses were the first scientists to initiate a plant study at Mount St. Helens. Fifteen months after our first venture into the debris plain, A.B. and Virginia again returned under sponsorship by Earthwatch, which provides support for scientific expeditions around the globe. This time, Earthwatch volunteers made up most of the Adamses' eleven-person crew. Some volunteers had paid $800 to join the project. Others had won Earthwatch trips as part of scholarships. Still others in the group weren't part of Earthwatch but signed up because they had their own research study going on or just wanted to help the Adamses. Virginia, who had added the University of Puget Sound to her teaching load that still included PLU and UW, had previously finished her half of the research effort, so she was not along on this hike. A.B. was on the ground wrapping up his. When he led the group on a three-hour hike over the rugged wasteland terrain on a September day in 1983 to Studebaker Ridge, he was joined by two UW seismologists eager to check out an earthquake-monitoring station atop the ridge. The group was also accompanied again by news photographer Bob Rudsit and me. We trudged over rocks and ash-covered dead trees and in and out of deep canyons carved by flowing debris.

Arriving at Studebaker Ridge, just over a mile from the volcano, it was amazing to see plants standing out like an oasis on a desert of volcanic rocks and ash. These ridge plants survived the volcano's massive lateral blast that destroyed much of the landscape five or six miles north of the mountain. A.B. said they survived because they were on a north-facing slope that protected them from the force of the explosion. The plants also were covered by a heavier layer of snow than other areas because the ridge faces north. "The snow kept the plants cooler, shielding them from the hot lava and rocks that flowed out of the volcano on that fateful day," A.B. said. On Studebaker Ridge, there were willow and elderberry plants that appeared to be chewed up a bit. A.B. suspected elk; he later found tracks and elk droppings that confirmed his hunch. Other flora recorded on the ridge included false dandelion (*Hyrochaeris radicata*), ragwort (*Senecio sylvaticus*) and monkey flower (*Montia siberica*).

Botanist A.B. Adams looked at one of the many ponds created on the debris plain. *Author's photo.*

Bob Rudsit surveyed the stark landscape. *Author's photo.*

The Adamses had already recorded about 230 species in their study and fully expect the nearly 300 species common to the region would return. In the devastated volcanic zone, they and their volunteers planned to install more plots with seed traps to catch windborne seeds, adding to the several dozen plots they initially placed. Their data was showing that Noble fir seedlings had increased tenfold in the past year, likely due to a cooler summer and more rainfall during the year. A mixed forest was possible if the Noble fir continued to grow in numbers, as have Douglas fir and Western hemlock. That, insisted A.B., could greatly improve chances of wildlife and fish being reestablished.

The volunteers had the times of their lives. Don De Angelis, thirty-nine, an ecologist with the Oak Ridge nuclear energy research facility in Tennessee, said the field work at St. Helens would help him in his job. Students Chris Chan of Los Angeles and Cathy Shin of Philadelphia, at the volcano on scholarships, said the experience was educational and exciting. Howard Haemmerle, thirty-one, a computer maintenance worker for the *Tacoma News Tribune*, was helping out while gathering data for his own independent educational project at the University of Puget Sound.

The seismologists had an interesting situation, as Jim Zollweg explained. He was pleased that hiking into the ridge was a feasible means of checking on equipment. In this case, he had heard a report that the cable from the seismic instrument and batteries was not connected to the antenna. "I didn't believe that could be possible," Zollweg said, "because we were still getting a signal." As Zollweg traversed the top of the ridge to the seismic site, he still was certain that the cable must be connected, that the report was a mistake.

When he got close enough to see, he was surprised. The cable was unhooked. "I don't know how we've been getting a signal!" he exclaimed. "This is like something out of the *Twilight Zone*." Later, however, he concluded that the metal element on the end of the cable probably was transmitting a signal and that there was just enough power for the signal to reach Elk Rock several miles away, where it was amplified through UW's statewide telemetering system. Anyway, he fixed the problem.

The following year, in the spring, I believe, A.B. asked me if I wanted to hike into the blast zone around St. Helens on a weekend to help him check on the plants. Immediately, I accepted. This did not result in a news story, but I was more than happy to go because I had established a friendship that went beyond merely scientist and newsman. A.B. drove on a Forest Service road that got us to the west side of the volcano. Daylight was fading and nighttime quickly chasing away any remaining rays. With backpacks full of clothing, food, tent, water and other essentials, we headed off across irregular terrain. We didn't even need our flashlights; a full moon was providing all the light we needed. It was a strange, eerie feeling that came over me, and likely A.B. too, of a symbol of hope shining on us in the midst of a dead land, even though I knew better, having seen life returning in the study by A.B. and Virginia. But it sure seemed dead in the stillness of the night.

The next day, I helped A.B. check out the plots on the landscape, and I noticed two insects, both grasshoppers, making the best of their situation on the devastated plain north of the volcano. They, like us, were moving forward at this place and time. Perhaps it seemed odd that I recalled a quote by my favorite U.S. president, Teddy Roosevelt, and applied it to insects and humans progressing together, but I did. He said, "Do what you can, with what you have, where you are." And this wasteland was where we were.

HARVESTING DOWNED TIMBER AND REPLANTING SEEDLINGS IN VOLCANO'S SHADOW

Downed trees were blown over in a willy-nilly fashion for miles, lying there in what appeared to be a giant-sized game of pickup sticks after the catastrophic eruption of Mount St. Helens on May 18, 1980. How do you salvage more than 4 billion board feet of timber before it rots? Bark beetles were already ravaging the trees two months after the eruption. There was an incredible urgency to recover as much timber as possible. The Weyerhaeuser Company had approximately 1.25 billion board feet of timber on sixty-eight thousand acres within the blast zone around the volcano. The remainder of the board feet total was on U.S. Forest Service land. On Weyerhaeuser land, thirty-six thousand acres contained mature trees and twenty-six thousand acres had very young trees. About six thousand acres included meadows, lakes, streams and land being prepared for replanting. The timber company's monumental task, driven by the desire to recoup investment in its cash crop, began within two months of the destruction and continued until late 1982. In the end, crews salvaged 850 million board feet of timber—enough to build eighty-five thousand three-bedroom homes. The Forest Service managed to save about 250 million board feet of timber on ten thousand acres.

Halfway into the salvage operation, Weyerhaeuser helicopter pilot Jess Hagerman flew me, news photographer Bob Rudsit and *Tacoma News Tribune* editor Don Pugnetti into an area near the Green River north of the mountain. Joining us was Jack Wolff, the company's vice president for land and timber. We landed near an area that had been reseeded with Douglas fir. Hagerman was a pilot of some renown, having flown rescue missions for the National Guard after the devastating eruption. When officials wanted

Numerous blown-down trees were visible on the peak's west side, as was a logging road along a ridge in the background. *Author's photo.*

It was amazing to see such huge trees snapped so easily by an incredible force. *Author's photo.*

A Weyerhaeuser helicopter landed near where replanting was taking place. *Author's photo.*

to halt searches, he argued to continue flying into the blast zone to look for survivors and won. As a result, one of his missions resulted in the rescue of two contract loggers who had been working for Weyerhaeuser near its Camp Baker logging facility. That facility was destroyed by raging mudflows down the Toutle River.

The salvage operation was like nothing Weyerhaeuser had ever done before. Wolff called it "unique" because of the havoc the volcano had wreaked. It was difficult because of logistics of logging, flood control problems and restoration of the land to make it usable for future commercial crops. The site of the gigantic salvage effort was testimony to the uniqueness. The downed logs were scattered in Spirit Lake and on hillsides like fallen wooden toy soldiers in a make-believe valley of death. Other dead trees were standing like ghostly sentinels guarding a gray graveyard of volcanic ash. In this strange otherworld-like setting of the red zone, nearly one thousand loggers were working in the shadow of St. Helens. Each day, about six hundred truckloads were hauled out—some on roads constructed out of nothing, others that had to be rebuilt—and taken to two sorting camps along the Toutle River before shipment on rail cars to the plant in Longview. From Longview, the timber was made into lumber and sold mostly to Pacific

Right: *Tacoma News Tribune* editor Don Pugnetti took a photo of the barren landscape during a Weyerhaeuser-planned visit. *Author's photo.*

Below: *Tacoma News Tribune* photographer Bob Rudsit shot an image of timber-laden Spirit Lake. *Author's photo.*

Northwest markets. Logs larger than twenty-seven inches in diameter were exported to Japan. Before the eruption, Camp Baker was averaging four hundred truckloads a day.

Immediately after harvesting the downed trees, seedlings were planted in a restoration effort. Longtime Weyerhaeuser forester Dick Ford, who had worked at Camp Baker, was one of the heroes of that effort. Retired, he told me recently that they didn't have to worry about erosion. "We never see that," Ford explained, "because we leave branches on the ground to intercept water and prevent erosion."

Ford put to rest for good one bit of information about wood from St. Helens, confirming it was a fact that some of the downed timber made its way into the framed dome of the Tacoma Dome, a major sports and concert venue in Tacoma, Washington, that opened in 1983 following two years of construction. "How much wood I'm not certain and where it is within the structure I don't know," Ford said in 2019. The Tacoma Dome is billed as one of the largest wood-domed structures in the world.

Wolff said in 1981 that the "romance" of working near St. Helens had diminished considerably among the spartan logging crews. Their work, in this situation, had become just a taxing job, even with the bonus pay above their normal rate for working adjacent to an unpredictable mountain while worrying about a smoldering volcano with no one certain what it might do. "It became a tough, demanding job, made even more demanding than a normal logging job because of tough conditions," Wolff recounted to me on that November day. "They're working in that cotton-pickin' ash, and depending on the weather, the ash could be blowing around or it could be wet muck."

The downed timber was not a normal operation for foresters, who usually fell trees. That caused some problems in removal. Because of the gritty, abrasive characteristic of ash, embedded in the timber by the force of the eruption, equipment experienced greater wear. Trucks and other such vehicles were protected from serious problems by their filtering systems, but ash was sucked directly into chainsaws. The chains themselves also took a beating. Loggers would normally sharpen their chains two to four times a day. That doubled for those in the St. Helens red zone. Besides equipment, there was concern for people working in the area. Workers wore respirators to keep ash out of their lungs. Their health was closely monitored. Every six months, tests conducted on them were compared with a control group in Coos Bay, Oregon. A year and a half into the salvage work, there was no evidence of adverse effects.

Psychological effects were another matter. Wolff said some workers took leaves of absence because they "couldn't cope with looking down the muzzle of a gun," a direct reference to St. Helens. "I'm not sure why they felt that way," he added. "Maybe they knew people who lost family members or homes." Surveying the area being logged north of the volcano, Wolff admitted that thoughts about what the mountain had done crossed his mind. The gray, primal environment—like a moonscape—was a far cry from the green wooded environment with abundant wildlife to which loggers are more accustomed. Occasionally, some animals, including elk, were spotted on green oases in the midst of the volcano's wasteland. But mostly, the landscape looked lifeless.

Wolff said the company utilized research done by the Japanese on the volcanoes in that country and applied some of the Japanese strategies on post-eruptive reseeding, along with some Weyerhaeuser-generated ideas. The reseeding was going on simultaneously with the salvaging and continued for five years after that harvesting effort ended. For instance, the Douglas fir trees on the Green River area were planted deep so the roots extended below the layers of ash, thus permitting the roots to get nitrogen from the soil. In addition, Sitka alder, which releases nitrogen into the soil, were planted alongside, Wolff said, to "see if that will be a compatible situation." A special device, a scarification blade, was attached to a bulldozer to break up soil—mixing ash with the soil—before planting trees. One place where that was done was at the destroyed Camp Baker facility.

Dick Ford proved to be one of the key leaders of the land restoration effort. A month after the eruption, Ford and three coworkers shoveled through layers of ash to plant the first seedlings in the blast zone. They were concerned how the young trees would fare. While ash contains few nutrients, the trees were planted deep, and ash would hold moisture and prevent growth of weeds. Ford learned through a test—planting some trees directly into the ash and others in soil and ash mixed together—that those in the mixed soil/ash had a better survival rate. Ford was motivated to do the job, having worked for Weyerhaeuser's Camp Baker district at the large tree farm the company had operated there for one hundred years. For seven years after the blast, Ford oversaw crews that planted 18.4 million trees, mostly Douglas and Noble firs native to the Cascade Mountain slopes of Washington State, but also lodgepole pine and black cottonwood.

The replanting effort was called "regeneration," a term that Ford said came into use by Weyerhaeuser after the devastating fire of September 1902 in southwest Washington, a blaze that came to be known as the

Dick Ford, a veteran Weyerhaeuser forester who volunteers at the Forest Learning Center, explains an exhibit to visitors. *Author's photo.*

Yacolt Burn after the town near where it erupted. The fire swept across thirty miles. "Regeneration meant everything that happened with regard to the rebirth of the land—from hand seeding to letting it return naturally," he said. As a result of the fire, 230,000 acres of forest and farmland were left smoldering and ten billion board feet of prime timber were damaged or destroyed. Eighteen people lost their lives. Thirty rural families were burned out.

The timber company swapped a third of its land in the blast zone for public-owned land during formation of the Mount St. Helens National Volcanic Monument in the early 1980s. The replanting occurred on forty-five thousand acres Weyerhaeuser retained inside the zone's boundaries. The Coldwater and Johnston Ridge visitors' centers are part of the monument, on land formerly owned by Weyerhaeuser. A milestone of sorts was reached in 2005, nearly a quarter of a century after the first replanting in the Green River north of the volcano, when some trees were thinned out. This forestry practice, said Ford, will allow for the first harvesting of Douglas fir trees in 2020 in an area once so scarred that no one would have thought that anything would ever grow there again. "Forty years is about the average time period to harvest after replanting of an area," Ford said. Some of the seedlings planted in 1981 have now grown into trees seventy-five feet tall. Trees planted in subsequent years—1982 through 1987—will be harvested, too, in their own time.

People can learn more about how forests are recovering from the volcano's devastation at the Forest Learning Center along Spirit Lake Memorial Highway (State Route 504), a visitors' center Weyerhaeuser operates in partnership with the Washington State Department of Transportation and the Rocky Mountain Elk Foundation. And who better to be its founding director when it opened ten years ago than Dick Ford, a key leader of the successful tree-planting endeavor. He's no longer its director, but he does volunteer at the center once a month. That's where I found him one day sharing stories of the return of the forest to the area surrounding Mount St. Helens. Personable and gregarious, Ford was a wealth of knowledge to those people visiting the center and seeing the exhibits. He showed me a display of a huge chainsaw that he said used a carbide-tipped chain in order to cut through the ash-laden timber. The wood was still hard to cut even after loggers removed much of the ash through a hose system that blasted the downed trees before cutting with water under high pressure, much like those used by firefighters. "With carbide chains we only had to sharpen them once a day," he recalled.

Carl McCrary doesn't remember his crews using any carbide-tipped chains on downed trees they were cutting in the blast zone near Forest Service Road 2520. "I set up four towers, and we began to dig the embedded ash from the downed trees and cutting them up, then trucking them out," said the veteran Weyerhaeuser forester while volunteering at the Forest Learning Center. On a huge hillside, his crews were managing on their own. He said he had a mechanic, Ray Manzano, who came up with an idea to keep the operation going better by having a place for doing maintenance on equipment, which was taking a beating in the ash. "Build me a building," the mechanic told McCrary, so he had his men sink four poles and use two-by-six boards to construct a shack that was thirty feet high on one end and forty feet high on the other. "We made it thirty feet long, split our own shakes and painted a giraffe on it and called it 'The Giraffe Pen.'" When helicopters were dropping supplies or food, the pilots were told to "look for the giraffe." McCrary said he was proud of his crew. "It was a tough job, but no one complained. They just dug in and did it." Timber was cut, loaded on trucks and hauled to the company's mills in

Longview or Kalama. McCrary recalled rewarding the effort of his four salvaging sites by shutting down one at a time over a number of days and giving the men helicopter tours of the devastation the volcano had wreaked. "It was a real treat, a surprise, and they loved it," McCrary said. He added, with a smile, that his greatest accomplishment was "my crews went home to their families every night, and no one was injured."

TOWER BRIDGE EMERGES REBUILT, OTHERS SURVIVED

Standing below the rebuilt Tower Road Bridge across the Toutle River north of State Route 504 on Tower Road seven miles east of Interstate 5, one gets a sense of calm. It is a far cry from the chaos that prevailed four decades ago when fast-moving mudflows destroyed the bridge at that site, along with other highway and railroad bridges. The river, known historically for rafting and kayaking on adventure-filled rapids in clear, white-foamed water, has today regained some of that earlier allure. But the water is brownish with ash and dirt that has continued to roil in the riverbed since the eruption tossed it there. Construction began on the new concrete bridge in late November 1980 and opened to traffic in late June 1981, according to the Cowlitz County Public Works Department, but additional work continued for several months until full completion. The first Tower Road Bridge, built of wood in about 1900, was eventually replaced by a metal bridge that was destroyed by volcanic mudflows in May 1980.

Rafting and kayaking trips on the Toutle River feature some entertaining Class III and Class IV rapids. Whitewater enthusiasts usually put in at the Highway 504 bridge and take out at the Tower Road Bridge. One particularly dicey spot is in a rocky gorge that got dubbed Hollywood Gorge when the 1937 movie *God's Country and the Woman* was filmed around Mount St. Helens. A highlight scene was shot through the gorge. The movie was about competing lumber companies. The brother of one company owner gets stranded on land of the other company owned by a woman. The plot of romance and business rivalry was accented by the stunning beauty of a virtually untamed wilderness.

The new Tower Road Bridge over the Toutle River replaced one destroyed by mudflows from the volcano. *Author's photo.*

Seeing the new bridge, as my son Keith and I did recently, causes us to think of what occurred on a day that obliterated it, destroyed the land and killed fifty-seven people. I took time to think about my newspaper colleague Kerry Webster, who was on the ground on May 18 reporting the devastation.

Webster wrote about an enormous flow of heated water, mud and debris raging down the Toutle River, toppling bridges and temporarily forcing closure of I-5 because of damage to the Toutle River Bridge on the freeway. That bridge survived a savage battering. The scene on the bridge at midnight was bizarre, as hurtling logs thundered like cannon against the steel sides of the span and car spotlights played on steam rising from the heated river.

"I wouldn't cross that bridge on a bicycle right now," said Emil Huber, then the state's assistant superintendent for bridge maintenance. The river was choked from side to side with logs and other debris traveling as fast as forty miles an hour. The impact of logs hitting the bridge could be felt several hundred feet down the roadway. "Feel her shake," exclaimed

The first Tower Road Bridge, a wooden structure, was built around 1900. It was eventually replaced by one that was destroyed by mudflows from the volcano. *Courtesy of Cowlitz County Historical Museum.*

Huber. A whole tree that came speeding down the river was stripped of its leaves and branches by the bracework of the bridge as cleanly as a celery stick. The trunk, unslowed, sped on. Occasionally a piece of debris recognizable as part of a house or mobile home would collide with the bridge. Among the debris left tossed on the roadway was a torn-off bed of a truck.

The Toutle River Bridge was inspected and cleaned of debris early on May 19, the day after the blast, and reopened to traffic, which moved slowly, sometimes limited to one lane. Heat from the volcano created an eerie mist hanging over the raging Toutle River, and spume tossed forty to fifty feet in the air completed a Dantesque picture. A police officer in the city of Castle Rock measured the temperature of the river at eighty degrees Fahrenheit shortly after midnight, saying, "No fish in there anymore, that's for sure." In Lexington, a low-lying area of riverbank homes between Castle Rock and Kelso, sheriff's deputies drove up and down streets calling, "Move to higher ground," through their patrol-car loudspeakers.

At one road junction, a stranded teenager begged for a jump-start for his dead car. "Oh, geez, it's going into the river and I just put new mag wheels on it," he moaned.

In Longview, city officials closed the older of two bridges spanning the Cowlitz River, and tugboats worked into the night to break up logjams as they appeared. By morning light, the river level had subsided, and residents were returning to their homes, except on the upper Toutle River, where roadblocks remained in force.

TRAIL RESTORATION AT MOUNT ST. HELENS UNIQUE ANYWHERE

When you consider hiking trails, you think of forest and mountain paths that have been there forever, well worn and loaded with millions of footsteps of history. They lead to a cabin, lake, waterfall or mountain summit. If that history is interrupted suddenly, what do you have? Well, that happened on May 18, 1980, when Mount St. Helens exploded in a lateral blast that obliterated all trails that existed to the north of the volcano for 150 square miles. What you had then, said Ryan Ojerio, southwest Washington regional manager for the Washington Trails Association (WTA), was "a brand-new blank slate to work with" to develop new purposes for new trails.

The WTA wasn't there at the beginning but has been involved since 1993, when it launched its trail program. It works in partnership with personnel from the Gifford Pinchot National Forest and Mount St. Helens Institute. The first trail-rebuilding efforts were done by U.S. Forest Service crews when the Mount St. Helens National Volcanic Monument was created in 1982. Francisco Valenzuela, who was recreation planner for the monument during that time, recounted that monument planners decided trails should allow visitors to gain insight into geological, biological and even cultural features of the landscape while protecting a fragile ecosystem.

The trails cover the lay of the land, offering varied levels of difficulty for hikers. Ojerio said the trails have been designed to bring value to hikers' experiences. The WTA has embraced a philosophy that Valenzuela and others advocated from the beginning: nature needs the help of humans to sustain it, and humans need nature to sustain them. That objective drives the effort to design and maintain trails. Sometimes the actions of nature impact trails and make them inaccessible, requiring continual work to maintain the pathways.

For instance, the Independence Pass Trail that leads to a view of the volcano from the eastern shore of Spirit Lake was designed to provide an easy hike. Unfortunately, when you have a trail built on sand, dirt and ash, you have potential for erosion or landslides. Ojerio said Independence Pass Trail has been closed for eight years due to "sloughing off the hillside," making the trail especially dangerous. "We're working to get it opened," he said. "It's on our wish list."

Meanwhile, there are trails carved out of a rugged steep slope, such as Mount Margaret a few miles away, that are designed for seasoned hikers seeking a challenging experience. The mountain, already worn raw by the force of St. Helens' epic blast, consequently is less prone to nature negating the peak's chiseled path. On that path, known as the Boundary Trail, there is one ten-foot-long spot that is particularly narrow along a ridge, Ojerio said.

One trail that doesn't call attention to itself is Butte Camp Trail through a lava field with fantastic views. Trail crews brought in gravel and dirt to create a path that winds its way through lava boulders. It looks like a trail that has always been there. It belongs. Ojerio said Harry's Ridge Trail, leaving from the Johnston Ridge Observatory, is a classic hike, offering views of the volcano, Spirit Lake and even Mounts Adams and Hood on clear days. In summer, the hills are alive with wildflowers. The Lakes Trail goes to Coldwater Lake, which didn't even exist before the 1980 eruption. The ancient forest that once towered there was blown down, and mud and ash from the volcano dammed up Coldwater Creek, creating the lake.

Many of the trails that were on the fringe of the blast zone incurred minimal damage, and through continued maintenance they still provide experiences of varying degrees for hikers. From the northeast, there are: Meta Lake, a short paved path that is defined by a young forest that survived the eruption by being under a thick blanket of snow; Norway and Bear Passes, offering views of St. Helens, Spirit Lake, other mountains, blown-down timber and wildflowers, as well as camping options; and Truman-Pumice Trail, descending into the blast zone onto the plains by Spirit Lake.

Looking for more adventure? The twenty-eight-mile Loowit Trail circumnavigates Mount St. Helens, presenting a real challenge in an otherworldly environment. Ringing the peak, it offers ambitious hikers an up-close view of the volcano from every direction. "I've hiked it," Ojerio said, "and it's a rugged experience on some of the slopes, where I had to

Crews working on Loowit Trail on Mount St. Helens. *WTA photo by Ryan Ojerio.*

pick my way carefully." So the trail is not for casual hikers, and those who attempt it should allow for three days to complete the trek. Water is sparse, shade almost entirely lacking and erosion of the trail makes for some harrowing detours. Those willing to brave the elements will be rewarded by the stark beauty of the mountain and the diversity of life returning to it. Hikers are asked to check with Monument staff before attempting the trail and to obtain the required backpack permits for camping.

Make no mistake. Climbing to the summit of Mount St. Helens can also be an incredible adventure. My sons, Keith and Gregg, and I have climbed it. Gregg took an incredible panorama photo from the summit, with Mounts Rainier and Adams clearly visible. The climbing trail's purpose is obvious: ascend 4,500 feet to the summit crater. The climbing trail passes quickly through a sensitive forest and then reaches a section of exposed basalt, which helps minimize the potential environmental damage from large numbers of hikers. Once above the rock outcroppings, the trail goes straight up the volcano's south flank without switchbacks. It's just one step after another, getting you to the top of the crater as quickly as possible. In spring, snow makes the effort easier as one kick steps up the slope. Snow is a lot more forgiving on feet and calves. In summer, one is more apt to walk on pumice, dirt and ash, tending to take two steps forward and falling one step back. The view is awesome from the crater with Mounts Rainier, Adams and Hood visible and a huge drop-off—1,300 feet—to St. Helens' crater floor and lava dome below. Permits are required to climb to the summit and are available online from the Mount St. Helens Institute after February 1 every year.

Ojerio advised hikers to check online at the WTA for trail information and to view the comments hikers provide on up-to-date trail conditions. There are numerous hiking books and guidebooks out there that have information depending on when they were published. "The best advice I have is to do some research online, but always be prepared with a back-up plan," Ojerio said.

Trail crews over the years faced great obstacles in creating and maintaining trails and will continue to do so. In the 1980s, they had to deal with entire forests that were blown down. They were reluctant to just cut up trees with chainsaws because they didn't want hikers to feel like they were walking through a timber tunnel. They used heavy winches to move downed trees out of the way or shoved dynamite into holes drilled in splintered trees and blew them out of the way. It didn't matter. Hikers would think the volcanic eruption caused the damage.

Today, it's a case of repairing damage so hikers can continue to enjoy this awesome wonder of nature. Ojerio is pleased to report, too, that more and more volunteers are stepping up to work in the field, which is encouraging, and he's always concentrating on finding grants to keep the trail work going strong. It's a worthy cause.

PART V

AFTERMATH

THE NIECE OF FAMOUS HARRY TRUMAN REMEMBERS

L iving at a Redmond, Washington retirement complex, Shirley Rosen today is older than her uncle Harry Truman was when he perished in the explosive eruption of Mount St. Helens on May 18, 1980. "I'm eighty-five," she said to me and my son during a visit in May 2019. "I'll be eighty-six in July." Truman, who was born in October 1896, was eighty-three when he died as the volcano's lateral blast destroyed his lodge at Spirit Lake. Rosen remembers Truman well, and the day of the big eruption is vividly etched in her mind. She wrote about that day and Truman's life in her 1981 book, *Truman of St. Helens*. Rosen said her sister Dayle called her about 8:40 a.m. and told her to turn on the news because Mount St. Helens had just erupted. She flipped on the radio, and she and her husband, Enard "Lee" Rosen, decided to skip church to listen to the news accounts. And to turn on the TV to see if there was any film footage yet.

When a radio reporter noted that Spirit Lake had disappeared, Shirley Rosen feared the worst. The report continued that the cataclysmic explosion was aimed directly at the lodge. She wanted to believe that Truman might have survived, escaping to his alleged hidden cave stocked with Schenley's whiskey and Coke for his favorite Coke-high drink. But the chance of living through such an immense, sudden blast seemed unlikely.

She got on the phone and called renowned University of Washington seismologist Steve Malone, with whom she had developed a relationship. "Steve," she asked, "how would Harry have died? Did he suffer?" Rosen said an empathetic Malone explained that the blast occurred very quickly,

Shirley Rosen holds a picture of the May 18 eruption of Mount St. Helens. *Author's photo.*

as evidenced by the fact that scientist David Johnston, positioned on Coldwater II ridge five to six miles away, farther than Harry's lodge was to the mountain, only had time to radio to colleagues, "Vancouver, Vancouver. This is it." Malone told her that Truman likely only had time to turn his head to look at the mountain. Malone explained to Rosen that there was a sound, a blowout, the bulge came down, pressure sucked all the air out, there was no fire. Everything was obliterated.

Thinking about what time of day it was, Rosen speculated that Truman likely was "on his front porch sweeping it off." She couldn't believe he was gone. She busied herself trying to find something of Harry's, thinking it would somehow make things better. She searched to find the Christmas card Harry had sent the previous December. She found it. When she opened it, she saw the postcard of a pristine Mount St. Helens and Spirit Lake glued inside. She felt a sense of loss—Harry gone forever and the once beautiful mountain and lake now turned ugly by the eruption. She read the note, in which Harry thanked her for her card, wished her family well and stated that a bad winter was being endured with considerable rain, snow and wind.

Rosen became emotional remembering that Truman would never get her last letter, sent May 17, the day before the blast. She had waxed sentimental, stirring up tender memories of perfect summers working at the lake and good times with "Auntie Eddie and Uncle Harry." Although Rosen expressed concern for Truman's safety, she said she understood why he stayed at the lodge with all his possessions—cabins, boats, motor home and so on. "He felt his possessions weren't safe, that people would come in and steal his stuff," Rosen told me. She said her letter ended with a poignant thought of unending love for Truman. She said, "I wanted Harry to know that."

A memorial service was held for Truman in mid-June, and many people who knew him offered thoughts and stories. Rosen felt it was too soon after the eruption. She was still holding out hope, however futile, that Truman was alive in his secret cave with his stash of whiskey and Coke. Tiring of all the news reports about St. Helens and her uncle, Rosen turned her attention to stories she'd already written about Truman, and she wrote a few more about the Truman she knew when she worked at his lodge in her youth.

She was interested in learning about the Truman she didn't know. She bounced her stories off Wayne McGuire, an English professor she had during a course at Shoreline Community College in Seattle. He encouraged her to write a book. Armed with notepad, tape recorder and plenty of tapes, she ventured forth to chase down people who knew Truman in his early life at Spirit Lake. Rosen did just that and got enough material to write her book, which was published by Seattle's Madrona Press in 1981 in time for the first anniversary of the mountain's big blast. She was a literary star. The book was a hit because it captured the true essence of Harry Truman, a study in

Shirley Rosen has fond memories of her uncle Harry Truman, who died in the volcano's lateral explosion. *Author's photo.*

contradiction. Rosen said he could be kind, he could be mean, he could be sentimental or tough, generous or frugal. Most of all, though, Truman loved to be the center of attention. But he still had a private side, Rosen insisted, that just a few people could penetrate.

Her book created a sensation. Legendary TV newsman Tom Brokaw interviewed her. "Brokaw loved my book," she said with a satisfied smile, remembering the occasion. Rosen hit all the New York news shows, including *The Today Show* on May 18, 1981, and then she toured the country on a book-signing adventure. When the publishing company went out of business, Rosen was forced to "run around selling the book on my own." She did some travel writing to get some income. Then, there was a stroke of luck that took her off in another direction.

Rosen got the idea that maybe she could get her foot in the door figuratively and literally at a jewelry store that was selling items made with Mount St. Helens ash. Maybe she could persuade the owners to sell her book. It worked for a while, but later she got advice to approach "these young guys" at Busch and Slates, a Seattle business selling art glass, some made from ash from the volcano. She said she felt weird, "an old lady talking to these men," but they bought her pitch and made her sales manager. "I went all over the country and had artists that I represented," Rosen recalled. "And I focused on Northwest artists." Some of the artwork contained St. Helens ash. Along the way, she learned a lot about glass, gesturing to a variety of glass art displayed in her Redmond residence.

Her husband, who worked all his life for a sand and gravel company, advised her to join an investment club. She did, and that turned out well for her, as she bought stock in some up-and-coming companies in the 1980s, such as Microsoft. But things wouldn't have turned out so well for her (Rosen's husband is deceased) if she "hadn't written the book." It's not often you have a character like Harry Truman as your subject. Rosen was happy to share some stories about him, including a couple that didn't make her book.

"Did you know that he had a pet bear?" Rosen asked. "Well, he did." Rosen said Truman found this black bear cub abandoned and adopted him. The bear would follow Truman around like a dog. He loved that bear. One night, Harry heard car noises and the sound of doors opening, then gunshots. He ran out to the road, caught a group of men in the act of killing his pet bear and threatened to report them to the U.S. Forest Service. "Harry had a good relationship with the Forest Service," Rosen recalled. "Its officers would have done something." She says Harry was heartbroken that people would bail out of their car, take out their shotguns, kill his pet and leave it lying dead in the road. She remembers Harry telling someone, "It [the bear] was not a wild animal. The wild animals were the two-legged SOBs that killed my pet."

Rosen said Truman was afraid of the earthquakes that were shaking the area around Mount St. Helens as it ramped up for its big blast. She transcribed a tape of a conversation between Harry and *National Geographic* freelance photographer Fred Stocker on a night in May 1980 when Stocker was staying at Truman's lodge. "That's gotta be a 5.0 [on the Richter Scale]," said Truman. "Hear the tinkling of glasses? See the barometer swinging on the kitchen wall? That puts the fear of God in me. The whole damn building's rocking now." Stocker interjected, "It's coming off the wall."

Truman commented he'd put some tapes on his player piano and they could listen to some old songs. "'My Buddy' makes me bawl," Truman said of that song. "Reminds me of my days in World War I." Stocker was mostly listening as Truman rambled on and on about inviting folks to the lodge, eating, drinking, playing songs. "'Georgia Brown' was my favorite," Truman said. "There's something friendly about a fire in the fireplace and a kitty laying with me." Harry's wife had died a number of years before, and Truman was treating Stocker as a true blue guest.

Truman's best friend almost didn't become a friend at all, as Rosen recounted in her book. That person was the famous U.S. Supreme Court justice William O. Douglas. Rosen said her sister, Elaine, was on duty in the lodge on a summer day in 1953 when a man entered the lobby wearing a rumpled suit, tie askew and a squished hat on his head. He looked like just another fisherman to Elaine. And Truman, sitting by the door of the kitchen, was gazing at the stranger with obvious disapproval. Truman motioned to Elaine and told her to tell the man the lodge was full up, no cabins available. She did as she was told when the man asked, and she suggested he try another lodge down the road.

The man left, and a half dozen men drinking beers at the counter yelled at Truman, saying he had just turned away William O. Douglas. Truman shouted, "I'll be goddamn go to hell" and shot out the back door, jumped in his pickup truck and sped down the road. Truman caught up with Douglas as the justice was checking in at the other lodge. Truman apologized and said there was a mistake; they had no cabins, but he offered a nice room inside the lodge. And Truman said he had horses. That got Douglas's attention, and he apologized to the young couple at the registration desk. He followed Harry back to his lodge. And the rest is history. The two eventually went on their first horse-packing trip, and Douglas returned on other occasions for many more adventures in the Cascade Mountains.

Turning away from tales of Truman, Rosen reminded me of when we attended the 1981 premiere in Portland, Oregon, of the movie *St. Helens*, starring Art Carney as Harry Truman. She told me at the time that Carney didn't do a very good job of capturing the true Truman. "There were no cats. Harry had sixteen, but Carney had a dog because he was allergic to cats," Rosen said. "Carney exaggerated Harry's persona." I thought about that and wondered how that could be but then realized that Truman was more complex than Carney could have known.

Another actor in the film, David Huffman, portrayed a geologist named David Jackson, based on David Johnston, who died in the eruption. The parents of Johnston protested that characterization, saying that their son was never a rebel and certainly not a scientist who took unnecessary risks, as was depicted in the movie. Rosen remembers that the actors on hand for the premiere cheered and lifted bottles of champagne when their names or characters were shown on the screen. She also remembers the after-film party on a Portland hillside and her car being anchored in the theater parking lot until she could convince officials to unlock it because she was an important attendee of the premiere.

As my son Keith, who was taking photos of Rosen, and I got ready to leave, she insisted she wanted us to examine a photo of a virgin Mount St. Helens before eruption with an elk in the field, and then she was going to buy us lunch in the retirement complex dining room. That gave us time to converse some more and learn that Turner Broadcasting had come to her place and interviewed her several days prior to our visit for a documentary it plans to air in 2020, the fortieth anniversary of the volcano's thunderous eruption.

VIRGINIA DALE DEVOTED TO STUDYING PLANT REGENERATION AT MOUNT ST. HELENS

Renowned botanist Virginia Dale takes the cake, literally and figuratively. A mother and a grandmother, she makes a volcano cake to die for. The cake symbolizes her forty-year research mission to tell the world about the resurrection of plant life on the devastated debris flow north of Mount St. Helens. She's also an award-winning biology ecologist. Virginia, who has a PhD in mathematical ecology from the University of Washington, was among members of the international science community that contributed to the International Panel on Climate Change Scientific Assessment that in 2007 received, with Al Gore, the Nobel Peace Prize. She received the Distinguished Landscape Ecologist Award by the U.S. Regional Association of the International Association for Landscape Ecology in 2013.

When I reached out to reconnect with her in 2019 after three dozen years had passed since our meeting on the plains of the volcano, I found her in Tennessee. She had recently retired from a long career at Oak Ridge National Laboratory, where she served as director of the Center for BioEnergy Sustainability.

She is still an adjunct professor in the Department of Ecology and Evolutionary Biology at the University of Tennessee. She enjoys being a mom to her daughter, Wendy Adams. I remember Wendy as a young child, being raised by Virginia and her husband and Wendy's father, A.B. Adams, while conducting their study of the plants sprouting back to life on the gray wasteland left in the wake of the explosive May 18, 1980 eruption of Mount St. Helens. When Virginia and A.B. divorced in 1984, she said, she moved to Tennessee. A.B. stayed for some years in Seattle. His family eventually moved him to Tennessee. "A.B. was physically well," Virginia told me, "and still is, but he was having memory issues, so his family—he has a big family—brought him home. It's working out well, they don't know what it is [mental problems]. It's hard for him, but he does remember St. Helens and likes to talk about it. The volcano had an impact on his life, and mine, too."

Before getting around to learning about her findings on the volcano springing back to life, I had to ask her about the volcano cake. She makes the cake with her daughter and son, Brad Hensley, all while relishing retirement with her husband, Keith Kline, and grandchildren. In fact, Virginia frequently joins Wendy and sometimes Wendy's daughter, Lilias O'Shea (her granddaughter), to lecture to grade school students. And they bring along the volcano cake.

"The cake has complex geologic features," Virginia explained. "It is underlain by a strawberry sheet cake that represents magma. Sometimes I put a layer of berries on top. Then, I add chocolate icing (the soil). The mountain itself is a chocolate zucchini cake. Gummy bears buried in the cake represent animals killed during the eruption. The mountain is covered with chocolate in the lower elevations, but white icing on top represents the glaciers. I like strawberries, so they are the lava. Pretzels symbolize the blown-down trees. Small herbs, such as thyme and parsley, depict the reestablishing vegetation." Virginia said she and Wendy serve the cake to youngsters and they really enjoy it. She's even prepared it for adults. "Yeah, I've served it at events like Pint of Science where scientists lecture at local breweries, which always manage to choose a beer that goes well with the cake."

Virginia had an instrumental role in the production of the book *Ecological Responses to the 1980 Eruption of Mount St. Helens*, which synthesized the research that had been conducted for twenty-five years since the eruption. She was author of some of the content and served as editor, along with Frederick Swanson and Charles Crisafulli, geologist and ecologist, respectively, with the U.S. Forest Service. Virginia's daughter, Wendy, who aided her mother over the years on research trips to the mountain, is listed in the book as a contributor.

"The plant life came back extremely well," Virginia noted. "All the conifers came in. Alder didn't come back right away; it needed wet soil." But alder has a short life span, and she expects much of that species to eventually die, increasing the potential for a conifer forest on the debris-avalanche deposit area north of the volcano. That forest will be dominated, she said, by Douglas fir, Pacific silver fir and western hemlock. "I thought

Above: Virginia Dale with her son, Brad Hensley (*left*), and her husband, Keith Kline, during a visit to the Pacaya Volcano in Guatemala. *Courtesy Virginia Dale.*

Left: Wendy and Virginia get ready to serve a volcano cake to students. *Courtesy Virginia Dale.*

the alder would die out five years ago," she mused, "when there was an infestation of tent caterpillars." But alder trees are still there, and as long as they are, they will be of value because alder is a nitrogen fixer, releasing that element to increase the soil's fertility. That helps conifers, which need nitrogen to flourish. Future disturbances will influence plant growth and rates of succession, disturbances that include potential volcanic activity; erosion and deposition; and mudflows associated with heavy rainfall.

"It's an interesting time now to look for changes," said Virginia, who will make her regular pilgrimage in late summer or early fall of 2020 to check on the plots she has been studying since almost immediately after the 1980 eruption. Change will be the primary theme during the coming decades on what is a dynamic landscape surrounding the volcano. "I anticipate the landscape will continue to develop toward a complex mosaic of vegetation patch types," she said, "but that woody species, particularly shrubs, will become increasingly abundant, eventually cloaking most of the landscape."

However, she added, a variety of coniferous and deciduous trees will likely emerge from the shrubs, giving the landscape an "open parkland-forest appearance." During subsequent stages of succession, streams and lakes are expected to become more heavily shaded as conifers become more abundant. And when, not if, a major volcanic disturbance occurs, the landscape will have a familiar look to it. "We expect that many biotic, landform and soil legacies of the 1980 eruption will be evident several centuries in the future," Virginia predicted.

Ecological Responses noted that animals have rebounded, too. Roosevelt elk made an astounding comeback within five years of the eruption and are still maintaining numbers. The effort is largely due to the work of the Washington State Department of Fish and Game, the Weyerhaeuser Company and the Rocky Mountain Elk Foundation. Those three entities developed winter-range foraging areas, planting pastures of grasses and legumes. But in areas without the seeding, abundant natural forage developed from re-sprouting plants that survived the eruption and from plants established from windblown seeds. Other animals returned, as well, including mountain goats.

The primary arthropod colonist of the debris plain was beetle families. "Why should that surprise us?" Virginia mused. "Wasn't it Darwin who said, 'beetles will inherit the world'?" During the study for the book, more than 27,000 beetles were collected representing 279 species and 39 families.

Historically, no other region of Washington State supported as many native freshwater and anadromous species of fish as did the region near Mount St. Helens. Thus, it was important to learn if the fish could come back after the eruption. Those fish included Coho salmon, Chinook salmon, Sockeye salmon and various species of trout. Fish rebounded more rapidly than expected because plankton and insects relied on for food also came back quickly, and in many stream channels fine sediment from the eruption was flushed during high flows so original gravel-cobble streambeds recovered in less than five years. Fast-growing deciduous trees, such as red alder and willow, provided shade to moderate stream temperatures. Beavers have been seen building lodges in ponds. Small mammal species noted at various oasis sites on the volcanic landscape include northern water slew, Richardson's vole, Pacific jumping mouse, deer mouse and yellow-pine chipmunk.

Virginia and other scientists will continue to study Mount St. Helens. That's why she's returning to the volcano in 2020, and possibly for more years to come. But she hopes a new wave of scientists will eventually step up to continue the effort. Washington's volcano has become one of the most studied, earning an important place in public education throughout the world. Many ecology textbooks present examples from Mount St. Helens. Scientists have become important commentators during major anniversaries marking the May 18 eruption. Print and TV media cover news of new geological and ecological changes at the volcano. People crave the mountain's story. When people have that kind of appetite, they need someone to fulfill the desire. That's Dr. Virginia Dale, who makes volcano cakes.

CLIMBING ST. HELENS' SOUTH SIDE POST-1980 ERUPTION

Climbing the south side of Mount St. Helens is a hard one-day effort, but it behooves you to get your permit in advance and to go down the night before to camp near the base of the mountain. Refreshed by a night's sleep, not having to get up early to drive to the peak, you can begin your ascent at the Climbers' Bivouac at roughly 3,700 feet. Those in good physical shape should be able to reach the summit after four to five hours, gaining more than 4,500 feet. Today, the summit height is 8,333 feet, having lost 30 feet due to erosion and rim wall collapse since 1980.

When I climbed it in the early 1980s, I was part of a group that hiked to the top in the spring with snow still on the mountain's flanks. Leaving the Bivouac, we made our way through a forest for a little over two miles, gaining about 1,000 feet of altitude. We attained Monitor Ridge and made our way through a field of boulders that seemed to take forever, ascending approximately 2,500 feet. Once on snow, however, the going was easier. We went upward and upward kicking steps to achieve the final 1,000 feet to the summit crater. Snow is much more forgiving on leg muscles and feet. We made it to the top in four or five hours. I can't imagine climbing it later than May or into summer. Scree for the final push makes it a "two steps forward and one step backward" kind of experience. The view from the summit crater was incredible with Mounts Rainier, Adams and Hood visible and the rising lava dome on the crater floor some 1,300 feet below us. Not venturing too close to the corniced rim was important, as we didn't

Gregg (*left*) and Keith Erickson on the summit of Mount St. Helens. *Gregg M. Erickson photo.*

want to take what undoubtedly would be a fatal fall to the floor. The descent back the way we came took half the ascent time, approximately two and a half hours.

My sons, Keith and Gregg, climbed the south side in 2009 and had no real problems. During their late spring climb, they were forced to deal with scree in the top one thousand feet of altitude gain, and it proved to be more tiring for their muscles, causing some fatigue that might not have happened on snow. But they made it. Gregg took an amazing panorama from the summit crater that captured a "photo of the month" award from Wikipedia and is still featured on that site. A year later, Keith took Graham Machin, a friend visiting from the United Kingdom, to the summit, and the Englishman was ecstatic about his success on one of our Washington mountains.

In addition to climbing mountains and taking panorama shots, Gregg has made a career—in between teaching assignments at Cal Poly in San Luis Obispo, California—of focusing on the dark sky. That mission covering ten years has taken him throughout the western United States and Alaska to photograph the dark sky. One of his amazing night pictures shows the Milky Way diving into the crater of Mount St. Helens. His dark sky photos are part of a video he is creating to call attention to the problem of light pollution, which is denying many of the world's inhabitants an unimpaired clear view of the night sky. Measures are being taken in some locations to mitigate light pollution in the United States and elsewhere. He insists there is much more that needs to be done. He believes everyone has a right to see a starry, starry night, wherever one might be, and particularly at special places such as Mount St. Helens.

WHAT WILL MOUNT ST. HELENS DO IN THE FUTURE?

As we celebrate the fortieth anniversary of the reawakening and explosion of Mount St. Helens, we wonder what the volcano will do in the future. We only have to look at the past to get some clues. Carolyn Driedger, geologist at the David A. Johnston Cascades Volcano Observatory in Vancouver, Washington, says in a matter-of-fact manner, "It likely will erupt again in this century and the next, as it did in the nineteenth and twentieth centuries." That means episodic eruptions resulting in pyroclastic flows, mudflows, lava flows and dome building. "We expect more of the same," said Driedger, who literally grew up with the volcano as her career blossomed from an intern in 1980 to a successful career that has included studying and remapping of glaciers in the North Cascades, assessing the hazards of St. Helens and other volcanoes in Washington's Cascade Mountains and orchestrating public education and news media outreach.

It's a career that wouldn't have happened if she had stayed the night on Coldwater II Ridge with David Johnston on May 17, 1980. She would have died, as did Johnston, when St. Helens exploded at 8:32 a.m. on Sunday, May 18. "It was a close call," Driedger reflected. "We all have to think about risks and make determinations on our own, especially as geologists excited about studying the reawakening of volcanoes." Even if there is no loss of life when a volcano erupts, she said, there are other things at risk, including humans' homes, jobs and possessions, let alone destruction of the surrounding landscape.

Carolyn Driedger has carved out an outstanding career in the past forty years working for the USGS on Cascade volcanoes, including Mount St. Helens. She is shown here in June 1980 on an ash mapping project near Blue Lake on the east side of the volcano. *Courtesy Carolyn Driedger.*

"People aren't used to dealing with volcanoes," she mused. "There is something unique about volcanoes, a sense of mystery. I mean stories about volcanoes have been handed down by Native tribes for hundreds of years. Even in the twenty-first century, volcanoes deserve our respect."

While Mount St. Helens woke up after a 123-year sleep, it took a bit longer for scientists to wake up to the way they monitor volcanoes. "In 1980, we had a single seismograph monitoring St. Helens," Driedger explained. "Now we have a whole network with site instruments called spiders. They can talk to each other, they relate information about earthquakes, land deformation and gases." She paused, then quipped, "Maybe they can even comment that they like the red jacket the scientist is wearing." Driedger may not be far off, given the advances in AI (artificial intelligence), smartphone and home-assistance devices, such as Siri and Alexa.

One thing is certain to Driedger, however. The advanced remote monitors allow scientists to see and receive data immediately. "The next reawakening we'll be able to catch right away," she said. "We'll know when there is magma or deformations. We'll know if there needs to be an evacuation or if it's nothing." Development of the new sophisticated, state-of-the-art monitoring devices means no one will have to be on a ridge watching a volcano.

"If we had had these then [1980], David Johnston wouldn't have needed to be on Coldwater II," she said. Scientists have "grown up," in Driedger's opinion, and are working more closely today with emergency management personnel at the state and county levels in Washington State. And they're doing greater comparisons with other volcanoes around the world, too, to get clues about what volcanoes in their neck of the woods might do. That helps them develop possible scenarios of activity.

Driedger noted that the most recent episodic eruptions of St. Helens have been from 1980 to 1986 and 2004 to 2008. Geological evidence shows that the volcano has had an eruptive history going back more than 37,000 years but particularly active in the past 2,500 years. Before 1980, a last-gasp eruption in 1857 resulted in pyroclastic and lava flows and dome building. That marked the end of a 15-year period of episodic eruptions.

Prior to that, there was an eruption of St. Helens that occurred in 1800, about which an old Spokane Indian chief named Cornelius told Charles Wilkes, leader of an expedition into Oregon Territory in the mid-1840s, that he recalled as a boy experiencing a powerful noise like thunder and seeing "dirt falling from the sky" and accumulating to a depth of six inches and causing his people to cry in terror, thinking the world was coming to an end.

Left: Between 2004 and 2008, Mount St. Helens emerged from a quiet spell to stage another phase of eruptive activity. *USGS photo by John Pallister.*

Below: More dome building was part of the 2004–8 activity. *USGS photo by John Pallister.*

Most of the volcanic activity creating St. Helens' symmetrical cone occurred over 2,500 years, consequently making it a young volcano in comparison to other volcanoes around it, such as Mount Rainier and Mount Adams. Eruptions of St. Helens were characterized by fiery, glowing avalanches, including one discharging to the southeast down a valley at the head of Pine Creek. Previously, lava flows seemed to play a minor part in St. Helens' development. But in the past 2,500 years, there have been huge mudflows streaming down valleys to the west and south of the volcano. One mudflow inundated the Lewis River Valley for forty miles. Several mudflows traveled thirty miles down the Toutle and Kalama River Valleys, according

Equipment on the summit constantly monitors the volcano's activity. *K.A. Erickson photo.*

Rime ice coats a telemetry station north of Mount St. Helens, where monitoring is a year-round effort. *USGS photo by Adam Mosbrucher.*

to 1970s research by Tacoma geologist Jack Hyde, who noted that some mudflows may have even reached the Columbia River.

One interesting development regarding the height of Mount St. Helens: Its current height is 8,333 feet. After the big eruption, the 9,677-foot peak was reduced to 8,363 feet. Driedger reported today's lower summit elevation, measured in a USGS survey, was the result of erosion and loss of rimrock by crater-wall collapses.

In the future, geologists will continue to closely watch Mount St. Helens. The volcano is expected to do more of the same, maybe even providing a surprise or two.

BIBLIOGRAPHY

Carson, Rob. *Mount St. Helens: The Eruption and Recovery of a Volcano*. Seattle: Sasquatch Books, 2000.

Columbian. "Mount St. Helens Holocaust—A Diary of Destruction." Summer 1980.

Dale, Virginia H., Frederick J. Swanson and Charles M. Crisafulli. *Ecological Responses to the 1980 Eruption of Mount St. Helens*. New York: Springer, 2005.

Farmer, Judith, Julie Harris and Richard Carson. *Mount St. Helens Volcanic Weatherbook*. Portland, OR: Mountain Graphics, 1980.

Harris, Stephen L. *Fire and Ice: The Cascade Volcanoes*. Seattle: Mountaineers, Pacific Search Press, 1976.

Hilton, Alice. "Our Mount St. Helens." *Cowlitz Historical Quarterly*. Kelso, WA: Cowlitz County Historical Society, 1980.

Holmes, Melanie. *A Hero on Mount St. Helens: The Life & Legacy of David A. Johnston*. Urbana: University of Illinois Press, 2019.

Jones, Alden H. *From Jamestown to Coffin Rock*. Tacoma, WA: Weyerhaeuser Company, 1974.

Kelso, Linda. *Volcano: First Seventy Days, Mount St. Helens*. Beaverton, OR: Beautiful America Publishing Company, 1980.

Mount St. Helens Eruptions of 1980: Atmospheric Effects and Potential Climate Impact. Washington, D.C.: NASA, 1980.

Olson, Steve. *Eruption*. New York: W.W. Norton, 2016.

Oregonian. "A Pall of Death Lies Heavy on Shattered Peak." May 28, 1980.

Parchman, Frank. *Echoes of Fury*. Kenmore, WA: Epicenter Press, 2005.

Place, Marian T. *Mount St. Helens: A Sleeping Volcano Awakes*. New York: Dodd, Mead & Company, 1981.

Rosen, Shirley. *Truman of St. Helens*. Seattle: Madrona Publishers, 1981.

Speidel, Bill. *The Wet Side of the Mountains*. Seattle: Nettle Creek Publishing Company, 1974.

Tacoma News Tribune. "Carter Inspects Devastation; Volcano Issues New Warning." May 22, 1980.

———. "Clearing Skies Promise Look at St. Helens." April 21, 1980.

———. "Dark of Night Hung On." May 26, 1980.

———. "Debris, Logs, Mud Destroyed Bridges." May 19, 1980.

———. "Eruption Erodes Volcano." April 1980.

———. "Folks from Afar Drawn to St. Helens' Eruption." April 1980.

———. "The Greening of St. Helens' Vast Gray Wasteland." September 4, 1983.

———. "Ham on the Spot Reporter Eruption During Last Seconds of Life." May 19, 1980.

———. "Harry Truman Blows Off Steam at Scientists." April 20, 1980.

———. "Life Around St. Helens Gets a Boost from Scientists." June 13, 1982.

———. "Mountain Rests after Puff." May 26, 1980.

———. "Mudflow Dam Fills Up." May 19, 1980.

———. "Special Report: Summary March to May." May 25, 1980.

———. "Truckers Slowed Dust Raisers with Blockade." May 26, 1980.

———. "Two Photographers' Lives Saved by Dinner Whim." May 19, 1980.

———. "Volcano Expert Calls St. Helens 'Dangerous.'" April 1980.

———. "Weyerhaeuser Flies News Team into Salvage Area." November 8, 1981.

Waitt, Richard. *In the Path of Destruction*. Pullman: Washington State University Press, 2014.

Williams, Chuck. *Mount St. Helens: A Changing Landscape*. Portland, OR: Graphic Arts Center Publishing Company, 1980.

———. *Mount St. Helens: National Volcanic Monument*. Seattle: Mountaineers, 1980.